THE INFLUENCE OF LOVE

LIFE EPISODES OF EMOTIONAL COMPLEXITIES AND RESOLUTION

NELLIE ONWUCHEKWA

We are all in search of our MATURITY EMOTIONAL NEST – decidedly or inadvertently. Only true love and positive emotions can transform a BEAST to a genteel soul.

Nellie Roselynde Onwuchekwa, B.Sc. M.ILD

American Journal *of*
Transformational Leadership

Printed in the United States of America (USA).

Cover design and book design *by* Anthony Obi Ogbo,
Production *by International Guardian*
Publishing: American Journal of Transformational Leadership

Disclaimer

The content of this book *"The Influence of Love"* is for general information purposes only, and must not be substituted for medical advice from a doctor or other professional healthcare providers. For specific questions about any medical matter, please consult your doctor or other professional healthcare provider. If you think you may be suffering from any medical or psychological condition, you must seek immediate medical attention.

DEDICATION

This book is dedicated to YOU, and serves as encouragement to all Men and Women emotionally traumatized by Deception, Rejection, and Betrayal in relationships, and impacted by a variety of emotional crises. You will surely triumph!

ACKNOWLEDGEMENTS

First and foremost, I would like to thank God Almighty for Divine Wisdom, Strength and Health throughout the writing and completion of The Influence of Love. In the process of putting this book, I realized how important this gift of writing is for me – to ease and emotionally vent. You have given me the power to believe in my passion and pursue my dreams. I could never have done this without unbridled faith in You. The Almighty God also surrounded me with men and women of inspiration. Thank you, Lord.

This work would not have been possible without the inspiration and tenacity of my three-decade plus old unconditional friend, teacher and senior colleague, Dr. Anthony Ogbo, author, publisher and Strategic Adviser of Houston Community College Systems. He reignited my writing skills and pushed for cruel timelines. Tonie, I am eternally grateful, but you were unbearably 'cruel' with tough deadlines. Thank you.

For supporting Emotionally Yours and Growth Café, which provided the background bases for this book, I am grateful to the following personalities whose influence spanning almost three decades have been fundamental in walking me through my emotional twists and turns: Prof. Peter Okebukola, Anthony Chiejina, Rev. Dr. Barr. Frederick (Freddie) Odutola, Reuben (Rubby) Onwubiko, Dr. Lawrence (Larry) Osa-Afiana, Dr. Levi Obijiofor, and Dr. Ogeri Azuogu. Auntie Ogeri, your 'sterling but crazily destabilizing' emotional thrashes were all worth it. Uncle Frank would be proud!

The following men indeed gave me a sure footing to that realm where emotional balancing and maturity must meet to texturize: HE

Orji Uzor Kalu (OUK), HRH Eze Joseph Anyanta, Chief Chukwu O. Chukwu, Chief Archy Ukonu and Chief Alex Ikwechegh Mascot.

To my children: Kennedy (Kenne), Stephanie (Stephie), Detra (Dee), Chinonso (Nono), Nitsher (Nasha), Crystal (Kris), Daniel, Alvin, and my grandson Adriyel (TamTam), you are the best gifts God gave me… I could never stop praising Him. You give me the emotional balance to manage and enjoy the thrills of motherhood. Stephie and Nasha: thank you for providing your youthful perspectives in making the book wholesome. To my dear sisters Ogechi (Ogey) and Nkechi (Nky), please remain the stabilizing factor that you are noted for. I thank God for my many adopted children for the opportunity to complete my emotional cycle.

To members of my Spiritual Family in the Seventh-Day Adventist Church, Nigeria, my gratitude for the foundational work done through spiritual nurturing. I will mention but a few as they are numerous to fill 100 volumes – Pastor (Dr.) & Mrs. Joseph Ola, Pastor (Dr.) & Mrs. G. A. Sholademi, Pastor (Dr.) & Mrs. Bassey U. Udoh, Pastor (Dr.) & Mrs. 'Leke Owolabi, Pastor (Dr.) & Mrs. Jacob Umoru, Pastor (Dr.) & Mrs. Emmanuel Ogungbesan, Pastor (Dr.) & Mrs. OPU Nwankpa, Mrs. Yusuf Imam and Chief & Barr (Mrs.) Godson Evulukwu. Of course, my Potters Outreach Family: the Dannons, Wrights, Obrimahs, Nwigwes, and entire members of this wonderful Bridge-building fellowship.

I am not forgetting foundational Apapa Church family where I took my first critical steps in life – the Osondu, Enwerejis, Egbulefus, Nmeribes, Nwogwugwus, Ubanis, and Marksons.

Working the complexities within Mobil Producing Nigeria, an ExxonMobil subsidiary, and surviving 20 years without any emotional or integrity scar was possible through the mentoring and coaching of many individuals, but a few stood in the gap, ensuring I walked the straight and narrow: Ibe Kachikwu, Anthony Okoro, Shuaibu Otori, James Ibe, Raymond Jones, Randy Broiles, Emmanuel Ogah, Ani Umoren, Onuorah Oji, Ita A. Stephen, Udom Inoyo, Oluseyi Afolabi, Gloria Essien-Danner, Adedayo Awobokun, Grace Oji, Adedayo Ojo, and Emeka Awobokun. I appreciate you all.

Along the pathway to emotional maturity, fervent and faithful friends hold your hands in the storms of life without judging you. I am blessed with many, but will mention a symbolic few: Athiel Greenidge, Craig McGowan, Samuel Otoboeze, Justin Ezeala, Mike Ndubuisi, Chika Ikem-Obih, Soibi Harry, Judith Mbonu, Stella Eze, Winifred Oyigah, Chinyere Udogu, Ide Owodiong-Idemeko, Elaye Otrofanowei, Joseph Nwakwue, Alero Eyesan, Patricia Opene-Odili, Afusa Alawoki, Emo Udobong-Ntia, Emenike Onwuchekwa, John A Agim, Obiamaka Onwudiwe-Lawal, Godson (GGV) Okorie and Lady Ifeoma Okali.

Posthumously, I salute my parents, Elder Ukaegbulam and Mrs. Mercy Orji-Chukwu, Engr. Frank Azuogu, Charles Bruce (a.k.a. 'Chaz B') and Uchechukwu Alvin Osondu. You taught me how to survive all emotional conditions and triumph, too. This book is based on part of many lessons you handed down. Sleep on my beloved.

Regards

Nellie Roselynde Onwuchekwa

Rendition of Emotional Complexities and Resolution

By ANTHONY OBI OGBO Ph.D., MBA, MMHR
Fellow of the American Journal of Transformational Leadership

Based on culture or traditional social environment, getting Africans to open up about their personal issues is an uphill task; getting them talk about their love lives may require special sedatives because the answer would be "over my dead body." Daniel Jordan Smith who did a gender related research about marriage and gender in Eastern Nigeria had a similar experience. In his study published by the *National Center for Biotechnology Information*, he wrote:

> "If it was difficult to get men to talk about marital sexual behavior in interviews, it was even harder to get women to do so, much less get them to discuss to marital monogamy after a history of premarital sexual activity. For obvious reasons, married women in the study did not volunteer much information about their sexual histories, even when the interviewers were socially skilled fellow women."

Therefore, it is remarkable on how the author of this book, *"Influence of Love"*, Nellie Onwuchekwa was able to create a mechanism for mingling with individuals mainly from this region, and sharing vital information about their relationships.

Not just that – Onwuchekwa's intervention strategy offers not just strategic solutions for long-term fixes, but also explains the emotional consequence of how the way individuals think or act to each other, and how the choice of self-centeredness could drive the development their relationships.

The language and challenges of love are universal, but the most complex. This book is not a reading novel but a study and collection of existential relationship phenomena dealing explicitly with realities of love and marriage. Lives matter with love and affection. According to Onwuchekwa, the influence of love is predicated on emotional maturity, stability and rationality; and propels the most successful relationships.

So how does the complex language of love harmonize the marital process? How could two or more incompatible individuals coexist to manage routine but conflicting engagements, congenital arrogance, and insatiable desires of live endeavors? How could age differences; family impoverishment, social, customary, and professional status interrupt the language and process of love? This book, *The Influence of Love* unloads a delivery of true-life events, transcribed to the core, to explain the actualities of love connection and practice. Not just those, the author, acquainted with the complex dialect and psychology of interpersonal affairs, confronts head-on, the emotional conflicts that devastate individuals, their relationships, and careers on a daily basis. As precautionary measures, chapters of this book share intricate relationship experiences and provide a thoroughfare for effective approach to managing individuals, their demeanor, and interaction with their significant others.

The Influence of Love...

By NELLIE ONWUCHEKWA B.Sc. M.ILD

Associate of the American Journal of Transformational Leadership

Man is a bundle of emotions. Our Emotions play critical roles on how we think and behave – and respond to stimulus or events around us. Emotions are what we feel everyday and they can compel us to take certain actions as well as influence the decisions we make about our lives. Our emotions can IN-FLUENCE our overall behavior.

Different interplays of elements impact our emotional responses, and influence the outcome of our relationships. Incidentally, emotions can be really complex, and, response to emotional stimuli – rational or irrational, may have life-changing impact on our lives.

We all want an opportunity for emotional venting. You will be surprised about the emotional conflicts that many people go through on a daily basis – and this has devastating impact on relationships and careers.

Over time we have come to the realization that unresolved, unvented and unprocessed emotions impact our health negatively – and relationships on the long run. Thus, the power of

Love Influence steps in as a stabilization tool for a rational emotional balance.

This book, The Influence of Love, brings the power of IN-FLUENCE in emotional entanglements, often referred to as 'LOVE' to the fore. This chronicle of true-life events, written in episodes, accentuates the powerful dynamics of INFLU-ENCE, which directly affects decisions of partners in relationships. Each episode reflects individual emotional struggles, conflicts, and sometimes, painful resolution processes. Of great importance is the author's key principle that "a relationship without invisible underpinning INFLU-ENCING variables is chaff at best".

The Influence of Love broadens the reader's perspectives and complexities of Love and Emotions, while strengthening the importance of principles, values and mores in crisis resolution.

It has been proven that LOVE INFLUENCE, which is predicated on emotional maturity, stability and rationality, propels most successful relationships. Enjoy exploring the depth of pain, emotion, pleasure and rationality that form the building blocks of stable relationships via the INFLUENCE OF LOVE.

TABLE OF CONTENTS

Introduction

Fidelity: Stabilizing Emotional Foundation
Let Us Walk Fidelity Back Home!

Issues – from sheer innocence to the lethargic. Sometimes discussions delve into frightening emotional depths that cast gloomy picture of their emotional lives from a futuristic perspective. While the word 'Fidelity' has various connotations and operational definitions, I refer to the 'ability to be faithful and committed – emotionally and sexually – to ONE person (your spouse or partner) throughout the period of your relationship.

Recently, I worked with a group of 80 final year students (21 – 26 years old) of a reputable tertiary institution on a special research project. Part of my objectives was to test their degree of fidelity or faithfulness and commitment to relationships. In turn, they were to test their parents/guardians (55 – 70 years old). My interest was to establish a behavioral cycle and determine if there is a correlation between the emotional patterns of the young people with that of their parents.

This piece is not about the research but some interesting variables arising therefrom. Fidelity or Faithfulness was not a strong feature in relationships x-rayed. Over 55% of the students believe "faithfulness" or "fidelity" is old fashioned and has zero effect on their current relationships. About 73% of parents/guardians had been 'overtly unfaithful'; 9% had left their spouses for another 'love', while 14% had constantly been 'mentally unfaithful'. Only 4% percent have been totally faithful to their spouses. Interestingly, the 'faithful bunch' were clergy and those 'survived' bitter divorces.

Five team members later met with me to share an emotional fear based on findings after group discussions. Their collective question is simple: ***Does that mean that Fidelity or Faithfulness should no longer be an expectation in modern day relationships? Is virtue of faithfulness truly gone?***
Of course, NO! Some people still believe that fidelity in relationships should be the woman's call… Men expect women to be faithful because it is an obligation. Truth is

faithfulness is an issue of integrity. It is a personal decision that individuals make in spite of wedding vows and verbal assurances. A man or woman DECIDES to be faithful regardless of his/her partner's lifestyle. The decision to be committed to your spouse/partner is predominantly dependent and propelled by the behavior of the other party.

Sometime ago, after deep meditation on the issue of faithfulness or fidelity going out of fashion, I held a soul-searching and dangerous discussion with the love of my life. Here's a snap shot:

Me: Darling, can you be TRULY faithful?
Response: Yes
Me: Can a man be faithful to ONE WOMAN?
Response: Yes
Me: What keeps a man faithful to his wife for the rest of his life?
Response: The Woman
Me: How? Why?
Response: The woman holds the key to the longevity of any relationship. She is supposed to be the mother, the confident, the nurse and the nurturer of any relationship....
Me: (Cut in) That is not fair!!! What role does the man now play? Are you blaming women for all acts of infidelity?
Response: No, my dear. A good woman pays attention. She knows when her son/daughter is straying or has emotional issues. It is the same in relationships. The woman has the GPS to keep the relationship on course.
Me: Have you been faithful to this relationship?
Response: Yes. I am TOTALLY emotionally wrapped, why

should I stray? Most importantly, I cannot hurt someone I love so deeply...

Above reflection is interesting and an innocent perspective on the issue. It may not be agreeable by modern women in relationships, as the quest for 'EQUALITY' has driven GOD-GIVEN roles of women to the background. However, it is noteworthy that there are elements of truth in the responses to the questions, thus, providing a unique element on the subject of fidelity in relationships.

I have no plan to open a discourse on whether a woman has more critical roles to play in navigating her spouse towards faithfulness. A peep into *Men's Health* magazine provides helpful insight to a man's tendency to 'stray'. A 2008 Gallup Poll indicated 54 percent of Americans know someone who has an unfaithful spouse. Also, the University of Chicago's General Social Survey "consistently finds that 20 percent of men cheat in their lifetimes, compared with 12 percent of women..." Today, the statistics are much more depressing.

If women can play a significant role in ensuring faithfulness of their spouses/partners, do they really understand WHY MEN CHEAT? Is it all about sex? No! According to Gary Neuman book, *"The Truth about Cheating"* out of 100 cheating men interviewed, only eight percent cited sex as the major reason for infidelity. Interestingly, 48 percent of them admitted that *emotional issues* led them to cheat. Thus, it can be safely established that it is not "just sex".

To Men: Beware of these signs

I am positive that before you entered into your current relations, love was at the foundation that grew the bonding into a pledge of loyalty and promise to stay faithful. However, temptations abound out there. Scott M. Bea, PsyD, a clinical psychologist provided the helpful professional perspectives below:

Beware When:

- • You are increasingly interested in flirting with someone new in order to gauge the possibility of establishing a more intimate relationship.
- • You have persistent sexual and romantic fantasies about a particular 'potential partner'.
- • You find yourself inviting or agreeing to meet or dine alone with a person with whom you feel a sexual or romantic attraction.
- • You are beginning to confide in an individual with whom you feel sexual or romantic attraction.
- • You have a history of infidelity coupled with a new opportunity to cheat.

To Women:

Help Our Men: Of a truth, I am yet to meet a man who sets out to be unfaithful in a loving relationship. Temptations, emotional stressors and other inexplicable circumstances drive them to seek 'solace' in the wrong barn. These 'temporary solutions' eventually end badly due to faulty foundations.

As earlier established, women are naturally gifted with emotional intelligence and always have a 'feeling' that something is wrong in a relationship. Women have God-given instincts for sensing when their men are in trouble. Women who truly love their spouses ALWAYS KNOW when their men begin to drift and can propel them lovingly back to the right track – without angst or vituperation. Please…

Discuss With Him. We have established that it is NOT all about SEX. Communication is the livewire of any true relationship. Effective Communication is the outcome of a deep friendship between the two people. Humour him and do not exasperate him with jealous remarks. Establish that you both have a problem and work it via a heart to heart talk. So, talk without being opinionated.

Ensure Intimacy. Intimacy is the result of a strong bond between people who truly love each other. Intimacy does not denote sexual contact. Physical contact between lovers is more than sex. Relationship experts say: "Intimate touch - from stroking hair to massaging to simply holding each other, is key to keeping those bonds strong. "Kiss, massage, and keep those loving hands on each other: This works on basic biological levels to keep people literally connected and respond to one another, to anticipate each other's needs, to look to each other rather than new, unknown partners."

Do you feel emotionally connected when you touch your partner?

Help Him Avoid potential cheating traps. Dr. Scott Bea established that most men know when they are faced with potential traps. Sometimes, steering clear of these situations may be difficult, especially when emotionally stressed. Do you encourage him to discuss personal challenges – or does he have someone else he is comfortable discussing with? Being open, and, understanding the frailties of your spouse/partner will help him avoid emotional booby traps that could lead to unfaithfulness.

You must understand the need to intimately discuss the dangers of meeting alone with anyone that he might feel attracted to sexually or romantically. Confiding personal details to anyone that he might feel attracted to sexually or romantically is a dangerous signal. "It's also a good idea to avoid or eliminate 'friendly' hugs and kisses." The same goes for new avenues of cheating, such as online chat rooms and other forms of social media communication.

Note:
Avoid making him feel cornered. Approach discussions of potential infidelity tactfully with clear display of love and concern. He must understand that both of you have an invaluable emotional investment, and, your desire/commitment to make it work.

Fidelity in spousal and romantic relationships establishes the basis of emotional stability and general wellness. It assures peace of mind and confidence in children. While it has been noted that both men and women have individual roles to play, the woman continues to hold the key and emotional GPS in keeping the man on course.

Women, let us get off from heights that hurt relationships. Let us invest emotionally in our relationships. Let us forgive mistakes and lovingly navigate our spouses and partners to the path of fidelity, loyalty and integrity. Stop impugning the reputation of the man before the children.

"…And the two shall be one…" means that when you repudiate your spouse before the children, you inadvertently drag yourself into the mud too.

So, let us WALK Fidelity back into our relationships…

Emotionally Yours,

Nellie Onwuchekwa

1

Episode 1

The Power of Love
Am I Being Fooled By My Emotions?

Sitting at my balcony on a beautiful sunny but breezy Sunday afternoon, after mild rain showers – with my eyes closed and enjoying every bit of the refreshing early afternoon weather, my staff tapped me with a very worried countenance. "There's someone at the gate to see you. She is not familiar…"

From the balcony I requested the security guard to open the pedestrian access gate to see my 'unknown visitor'. My worry was a total stranger trailing me down home; I was not at ease at all. Shortly, my guard said the 'visitor' refused walking through the pedestrian path, but insists on driving into the compound. Different security breach scenarios flashed through my mind, but something curious within me made me come downstairs to 'view' the stranger at the gate. Someone with criminal intensions would not wait patiently to be attended to…

Upon my approach, a beautiful middle-aged woman stepped out of a red sports car. I signaled for the vehicular gate to be opened, as I welcomed this beautiful, delectable stranger who wore a very distraught countenance. "Nellie, I need to talk to someone. I need a FRESH EAR…" she muttered and walked past me towards my sitting room. I calmly held her hand and took her straight to the penthouse where I have the "war-room-like office" far from the rest the house.

She made herself comfortable and broke down in tears. My beautiful stranger cried for more than 15 minutes, while I sat down shaken, wondering what load could be so heavy that would bring down this seemingly tough petite and obviously wealthy woman. I was jolted back to reality from my reverie by the most sonorous voice I have ever heard. Every word sounded like a perfect rhyme. Her voice would melt the stoniest heart…"Let me introduce myself. My name is Kandrea… with a 'K'. I am told I could speak with you confidentially. Please don't judge me…"

After the introduction and exchange of pleasantries to create a relaxed atmosphere, I asked if she would approve a recording of the conversation for my personal records, to aid factual representation of facts. She obliged. I further stressed that if her story could help someone in similar circumstance, I would need permission to share without compromising her identity. Kandrea was very excited about sharing her experience to help victims in emotional triangles or mess...

"My name is Kandrea; I am 54 years old. I have been in a relationship with a Clarence who is 35 years old. He is mature, loving and very supportive in coordinating my businesses. Clarence is honest and has over the last six years exhibited the highest level of ethics and integrity. He has never mixed business with pleasure; we always separate out personal lives from business. I hired Clarence 12 years ago when my late husband, Robert (Rob), became very ill and needed to delegate more. As a young Chartered Accountant with an International MBA, my husband and I felt we needed a young graduate with the energy required to handling drilling management and consulting business. With additional oil and gas management certificate, Clarence fitted the role and my husband took him in like a son...

"Yes, like a son, because after many years of marriage, we were not blessed with a child. We adopted my late sister's son, Harry, who is in High School. Thus, when my husband died, Clarence took charge of the business. Our employees respected him because they perceive Clarence to be the son I never had.

"Two years after my husband died, I suffered a heart attack and Clarence moved into our home – The Orchid Mansion –

to take care of me. Gradually, we both developed fond feelings for each other, which, initially, I regarded as 'unholy'. I worried about this strange fondness and love (still wonder if it was LUST) that was building so fast between us. I was conscious of the age difference, however, that fact became insignificant over time. My greatest worry and fear was the reality that I would lose Clarence someday. Unfortunately, like most people truly in love, propelled by hormones and other emotions, reality is often relegated.

"Gradually, Clarence became the "Man of the House" and "The Boss" at the office. My world revolved around him and his word became LAW at the Mansion and the Office. By Divine orchestration, his 'influence and activities' at the office required Legal processes. This made it mandatory that Legal Reviews were done before my signature in financial transactions. Clarence requested for proxy powers – in the likely event that I am indisposed to perform critical functions at the office. I wound lovingly affirm that I am very much around and God has promised me long life. Also, the Executive Vice President is my husband's bosom friend and junior partner in the organization.

"One Saturday morning, his family (including his Uncle, Maxwell, a personality of note) visited to accuse me of bewitchment. I was called unprintable names but Clarence stood in defense of whatever 'honour' I had left. They claimed that since he had been living at my home he had neglected his family. Maxwell calmly advised Clarence to pack his bags and follow them home. They demanded that I release Clarence from 'all enchantments'. He applied for Emergency

Leave the following week. I did not know that it was indirect severance from the company he loved and contributed a great deal to grow.

"This abrupt exit caused me serious emotional and physical stress. The situation was worsened by the news that Clarence had married his College sweetheart. It was at this point that I realized that Clarence was my life. I became suicidal and a hermit. Nothing mattered anymore. Clarence had buried the years of emotional commitment and love. Clarence never looked back. Years of emotional bonding, love, privileges and career had been thrown down the drain.

"After months of therapy, I recalled my adopted son, Harry from the investment company where he was working. Harry needed to take over his father's company as I was planning to retire at 55 to enable me focus on my health challenges.

"Six months ago, Harry came home with some correspondence for me. One letter caught my attention because of the very familiar handwriting – Clarence's. After days of hesitation and conflicting emotions, I summoned courage to open it – and received the greatest shock of my life. Inside the A4 size were undelivered letters addressed to me. A particular envelop had 'DO NOT BEND' across it. I carefully opened to see a Skeleton version of Clarence on life support in an intensive care. Another photo was of the most beautiful baby I have ever seen; behind the photo "KATHY" was inscribed at the back. A post-it note in a handwriting that seemed that of a little child read:

"I am sorry my love. Kathy is YOUR daughter. The wife they married for me died in the accident that has made me almost a vegetable. I managed to scribble this. Please come and take Kathy away. Call the number below. Forgive me. I still love you, C."

"Harry called the number and later drove me to meet the most adorable child on earth. We also visited the specialist hospital where Clarence was neglected for lack of funds. His family could no longer afford the bills and since he "had been confirmed a vegetable" they abandoned him to die. I wept uncontrollably at the hospital. Harry made some calls and Clarence's case was reviewed. Doctors told Harry that Clarence needed to be flown abroad for URGENT MEDICARE. I would need over $50,000.00 (Fifty thousand dollars) to restore and rehabilitate him. Clarence refused to accept treatment. He said this was God's reward for treating me badly. He URGED me, with all the energy he could muster: 'Please save Kathy; she is the child we would have had together. This is my Karma as I was not faithfully dealing with you all those years....'

Kandrea turned to me with pleading eyes, "Please tell me what to do. Pastors had condemned me to everlasting hellfire; my family labeled me an adulterer. No one saw my needs; no one felt my loss, my loneliness, and sad nights. My lame attempt at joy has turned the world around me against me. Without sentiment, talk to me..."

Honestly crippled by this emotional outpour of a woman I had connected with during this period, I poured her a cup of freshly brewed ice-cold ginger/garlic tea – with a background jazz mix to calm her. I needed something to distract me from everything I have heard, wondering what I would have done if I was wearing her shoes. While Kandrea sipped my special brew, I silently asked God to guide me in the interaction to follow.

What followed was surprising to us; Kandrea wept loudly and uncontrollably. Holding her in my arms, I realized how much she loves Clarence. In spite of her near-perfect composure even as she wept, I noted that Kandrea was in dire straits emotionally, and was gradually turning to an emotional rag doll – a mess.

After the emotional storm, I told her we needed to speak 'rationally' on the issue – if she was up to it. While Kandrea was eager to continue discussion, I calmly advised a reschedule – suggesting The Orchid Mansion to be venue. I observed her reluctance, but stressed that we needed to deal with the subject based on environmental realities. I was desirous to live her life through my mind and emotions. I needed to test the 'operating environment', which was to be the RATIONAL BASE for further discussions. To be exorcised of all the painful emotional entanglement, Kandrea NEEDED to work me through her life with Clarence.

Kandrea was clearly reluctant and vehemently opposed to the venue. We agreed to rest the issue until she was ready, because the matter required the highest level of confidentiality. As she was about entering her car, I asked like a petulant spoilt girl, "Kandrea, do you pray?" Observing her hesitation, I added, "Never mind, I will pray about everything. I need time to process everything…Please, do call me when you are

ready to walk me through your home." She smiled and nodded weakly like a child and her chauffeur drove off.

Three weeks rolled by slowly without a call from Kandrea.
I was full of anticipation whenever my phone rang. My mind
was a whirlpool of emotional analysis: 'What if'; "Why not";
"Supposing…" By the fourth week, I had filed away my
working note of "Emotional K", still wondering how she was
coping – emotional stress, work pressure and a quickening
conscience regarding Kathy.

Exactly six weeks later, I received a call at 0430hours to
clear a "stranger' at the main gate of my residential estate. I
worked all access control issues regarding 'ungodly hour visitors'. However, Kandrea was not planning on coming into the
home office, but directed, "why don't you get dress up for
that walkthrough..."

As I walked through Kandrea's beautiful and serene home
one hour later, I understood what she had gone through. From
the foyer through the hallway, living rooms, study, kitchen,
bedrooms, swimming pool, gym – including the garden had
the CLARENCE SIGNATURE!!! Every corner had a story
tied to Clarence. Harry, Andréa's adopted son spoke of
Clarence as "Dad". Harry made a "Freudian Slip", which
opened to doorway to openly discussing Clarence.

Harry talked about Clarence as if he was 'away on vacation'. He admitted he loves 'Dad' and enjoys copying his
fashion style by going through Clarence's wardrobe – and
sometimes 'loaning with mum's approval.'

A cursory look over at the wardrobe area indicated that Kandrea had continually bought gifts for Clarence all the years he had left her for another woman – Birthdays, New Year, Valentine Day, etc. I was shocked beyond belief. Surrounded by memories, haunted by disloyalty and perpetually conflicted, Kandrea was grinding her heart with hurt. This the foundation of her 'heart problem' – she was killing herself daily by idolizing and worshipfully keeping emotional memoirs of a love that long set sail to an unknown island.

Kandrea also realized that the time had come for us to discuss rationally. She naturally chose the Study to which I gently objected and requested we use the garden "to enjoy the early morning fragrance from the plants and flowers". She reluctantly obliged, but decided to give ALL DOMESTIC STAFF the day off, as Harry was traveling to another city with an early flight schedule.

At that point I knew she was ready to swim or sink through this tide of emotional mess. Kandrea was apprehensive when I brought out my notebook – not knowing the pattern the discussion would take. I decided to adopt a very intrusive path that would break her but help her wade through to a decision point as to what her next steps would be.

Below are the some key discussion areas and responses therefrom:

Me: What was the main object of attraction to Clarence?
Kandrea: Initially sex, but as time passed, I realized I

could buy sex. It grew from fondness to love over a period. I am not sure when love came into the picture.

Me: Did the age difference make you feel awkward?

Kandrea: Not really. I believe the intensity of emotion eroded the gap between us

Me: Were you comfortable introducing him to family and friends as your 'man', 'fiancée' or 'husband.'

Kandrea: Not really. People knew we were in a relationship. I did not care much about other people's opinion in my personal affair

Me: Why do you still have Clarence intensely present in your home after these years?

Kandrea: His 'presence' makes me confident of our love. I am steadfast in whatever I believe. To me the relationship was…No, IS the best gift the Almighty gave me and I intend to keep it that way. Clarence's behavior and betrayal is of no consequence when I consider what we have. His disloyalty dims to nothingness. I did mention earlier that religious leaders, family, friends, etc. have demonized me. This is the main reason I needed a non-sentimental 'third eye'.

Me: Your relationship with Clarence is in the past. Our collective focus is mending that heart…helping you heal. What do you plan to do with Clarence and Kathy? As you…

Kandrea: (Interrupts) My relationship with Clarence is not in the past. I may seem to be living in denial, but I have an opportunity to have a real family. So, I need your perspective without sentiments.

Me: (Thoughtfully) I cannot get past your emotional entanglement. It is difficult to process things without sentiments because you are frazzled by this walkthrough.

Two weeks later, after careful consultations, ***Emotionally Yours*** sent Kandrea a rational perspective to enable her take,

develop and implement an emotional roadmap without inter-
ference. The Executive summary is captured in the cover letter.

My dear Kandrea,

*I thank you for the privilege and honour to discuss very
sensitive and delicate matters of emotional importance. I am
deeply affected by the situation that has thrown you into an
emotional, psychological and spiritual traumatic state. Of
major concern is your 'conviction' that your feelings of unconditional love for Clarence remains unchanged.*

*The detailed evaluation analysis of the case are contained
in the folder, rationalized in four (4) possibilities, based on
facts and sundry realities with summary of perspectives for
your consideration:*
a)Medicare and Rehabilitation of Clarence
b)Kathy's Adoption
c)Reunion with Clarence – with Kathy (The Family)
d)Harry - The 'Invisible' Stabilizing Factor

***Medicare and Rehabilitation of Clarence.** Clarence is in
need medical attention and thus, needs your help. You already
offered to 'take a chance' with 'optimal medical assistance'.
You are conflicted and feel responsible for what happened to
Clarence. For this reason, there is urgent need for you to
emotionally exorcise yourself of this 'burden', which is prey-
ing negatively on your health. From discussions, you already
approved for your late husband's Foundation to handle; efforts have also been made by the Foundation to get Specialist
Review of the case.*

While we support your earnest desire to help Clarence, we STRONGLY ADVICE that you consult with his family before progressing your plans further. We know that medical intervention and eventual recovery of Clarence will untangle you emotionally. So, do it! If results turn out negatively, your conscience will be at ease, as you must have done your best to save "the love of your life".

Kathy's Adoption. *From your submission, you have already taken Kathy in for pediatric evaluation at a Children's Specialist Hospital. You stated your 'connection' with Kathy. That is good; however, you need to do the paperwork on Kathy's adoption. The note from Clarence, his friends' support and emotional connection are not legally binding. Please get an experienced lawyer immediately to evaluate the case and provide required guidance on the matter.*

The death of Kathy's biological mother does not mean that Kathy is alone in the world. Shock of the death of their daughter might be responsible for slow or seeming lack of immediate responsible and affectionate actions towards Kathy. Kathy's Adoption, if not well handled may lead to a messy legal tussle, and ultimately impact on your already tangled emotions and fragile health. Please tread softly and carefully on Kathy.

Reunion with Clarence – with Kathy (A Family?). *It is natural to live in perpetual denial of reality when enmeshed in webs of "may be' and 'could be', nevertheless, the truth must be told here.*

The Clarence you loved is NOT the same man. Clarence has gone through an emotionally traumatic loveless marriage. From that fateful day when his family 'dragged' him out of Orchid Mansion, he CHOSE to live a robotic life to please his family – as many "ONLY CHILD/SON" would act. He lost every resolve to stand by you when he came face to face with his family. Yes, Clarence loved you and could have defended your love and knitted heart, but he fell flat – without even a word – and aligned with his family. He deserted you without looking back and thereafter sought you out after the accident.

His family is his WEAKEST LINK. *Clarence seems like an intelligent man who has deployed emotional intelligence to his optimal benefit – particularly, after the unfortunate accident. No doubt, he feels guilty and regrets events leading to his bedridden state. Thus, you need to step out of your self-contained emotional ring and choose the right lens to view the current situation. Your mind and your heart are conflicted – you need to emotionally ventilate.*

Harry - The 'Invisible' Stabilizing Factor. *Harry is a wonderful young man who loves you worshipfully. Unfortunately, Harry seems not to be getting your attention, guidance, mentoring, coaching or mother's love. Harry lost both parents and knows you and your late husband as his parents. Currently, Harry has adopted Clarence as his 'dad' and works very hard to model his lifestyle and fashion after Clarence's. Harry has modified his desires to focus SOLELY on your happiness. Therefore, it is important that you balance that affection and make him feel loved too.*

*Harry is the **"Significant Other"** in your life, without whom any relationship with Clarence and Kathy could be a decided burden. He is the bedrock of your family unity.*

Kandrea, I personally noted a feeling of desperation in you, which may lead to negatively impacting and life-changing decisions. At 54, you are still beautiful and radiant. Please, DO NOT feel 'old'. Your life's happiness cannot be placed holistically on the altar of betrayal. Wealth and other forms of riches, unfortunately, do not assure anyone of Self-esteem – YOU INCLUSIVE. It comes from within – when you love and believe in your inner person – beautifully and wonderfully made.

Beauty is NOT the external picture or façade, it comes from within. We can work through your self-esteem, and together rebuild your emotional profile.

Always remember that the most important person in assuring your happiness and emotional stability is YOU. And, whatever decision you make, rest assured, we are here to support you…

Emotionally Yours

Expectedly, Kandrea called five (5) days after receipt of the comprehensive report and requested a meeting. I was determined to take control in order to navigate her to the right path. "Kay sweetheart, please take a ONE MONTH vacation. Let me be clear, and I speak now as a Friend. Leave the country to a place you have never been to. Do not go with the report. Go away. Ventilate. Reminisce about your childhood. Do everything but DO NOT THINK ABOUT CLARENCE AND KATHY. Direct the doctors and Lawyers on what to do. Please NEVER open any email. Leave a number for emergency with Harry. We shall discuss on your return."

It pained me to be so hurtfully firm on Kandrea who needed a shoulder to lean on. Sometime, you need to be firm and hurtful to achieve good results. I was glad when a cheery and youthful Kandrea called six (6) weeks later for update. I was not sure which way the pendulum would swing, but I was looking forward to the zestful, youthful Kandrea that called me for a business lunch at one of the most elegant hotels.

I was pleasantly surprised to see an excited Kandrea welcome me. She had gone to Barbados – a dream come true. She had wanted to visit that Caribbean country since she was in High School. So, we spent the first hour discussing her 'emotional vacation', while blaming me for 'emotional blackmail.

"Nellie, you opened my eyes. I did not follow through with your instruction because I took the report with me. I spent the first two weeks of my vacation emotionally ventilating and reading the report. I removed myself from the center and watched events from "outside the ring", as you put it. I am happy with the outcome and the next steps I will be taking…"

I stilled myself to listen without interruption, in spite of the desire to fast track the story to the "bottom line". Kandrea said Clarence had been flown abroad for treatment *(as a Charity Case),* while Kathy has been returned to Clarence's family. She took a personal decision to help Clarence from afar and treat his case like many other cases the Foundation had handled.

According to Kandrea, Clarence's family is repentant of their actions and very thankful for the assistance by the Foundation. However, she is determined to stay out of the case, because, "what will be, will be" *(Que sera, sera).* Clarence's family, without any intervention, appointed Kandrea Kathy's Mother and Guardian in line with their son's desire. Kathy currently stays at The Orchid Mansion with Kandrea…and she calls her "Mummy".

Clarence is progressing with treatment, but Kandrea has her groove back – with Kathy, her new source of joy.

Emotional Piggy Bank

Loving someone can sometimes be very hurtful, but you need emotional rationalization to help keep your head above the emotional storm. However, IF emotions are allowed to roam the domain of love 'recklessly', the results may be very unpleasant.

Love influences every part of the human faculty; emotions play significant roles in establishing the INFLUENCE of Love. However, we need a dose of rationality to stay above the turbulent tide of emotions.

2

Love: Strengthened in Weakness
Emotional Conflict: Is She Toying with Me?

Growing up, my father was my BEST friend and my **WALL of Gibraltar.** He was an easy-going sea-faring gentleman, who knew how to take care of ONE Woman – my mother. He was strong-willed and a disciplinarian and gave no room for excuses for failure. He was admired as he was revered by young and old. We never saw our father betray any form of emotion. We all called him a "Man of Steel". Each time we idolized my father, my mother would silently shake her head, and smile to herself.

One day, I returned home from school to learn that Mom was very sick and had been hospitalized. I accompanied Dad to pay her a visit, observed my father was visibly shaken, as he looked her over – with all the equipment connections. After the doctor's routine examination, my father knelt down beside my unconscious mother to pray for Divine Healing. Rather than say a prayer, my father sobbed uncontrollably – to my utmost embarrassment.

I rushed out of the room confused and devastated. To the best of my naïve mind, *"real men do not cry; real men are made of steel'.* Why would my father, an ex-soldier and an experienced seaman crumble needlessly? As the theatre of life moved me from one stage to the other, I realized that a man is as weak as he is strong. The strongest of men are known to be deeply emotional. In their love, men are also very weak.

This mental picture sets the scene for ***Emotionally Yours*** encounter with Kizito three decades later. A man of humble background, Kizito's education was made possible by a special scholarship contest. Kizito beat 1069 others to clinch the scholarship award when he was 21 years old. His sponsors, a multinational oil corporation, created additional requirement as key consideration for employment: students on scholarship consistently maintain an A Grade on at least 80% of his subjects throughout the four years of study. Kizito shocked the Corporation by sustaining a 100% A Grade throughout his study. Kizito, at 25, became an employee of one of the most prestigious multinational oil corporations in the country.

Today, 20 years later, Kizito, a very successful Chemical Engineer is emotionally troubled and conflicted.

When the multinational oil and gas corporation hired Kizito as a Star Employee. This placed him under immense pressure – loved and admired by some and 'loathed' by those who felt he was simply an opportunist. Some of the older colleagues felt Kizito was a product of 'favouritsm'. Irrespective of the faction, Kizito was a Controversy on Arrival. This misperception created a hostile environment and had an emotional impact on his ability to interact or socialize within the organization. He became a hermit and workaholic. His supervisors only admired him because he was productive and dependable. However, his social life suffered as he put in an average of 12 hours at work.

When turned 30, his friends from the university organized a birthday party for him at an expensive restaurant. He met Veronica, a Senior Sales Executive in one of the major Telecommunications Companies. They hit it off and got married within six months. They were in love and inseparable. Within five years of marriage, Kizito and Veronica were blessed with the arrival of three children – Vera, Kosi and Michael.

During their 10th wedding anniversary, Veronica suddenly became gravely ill and was rushed to the hospital for emergency surgery due to badly ruptured appendicitis. She died 48 hours after the surgery due to complications. Naturally, Kizito was grief-stricken and suicidal, but the awareness of the impact of the loss on the children held him back. Family and friends rallied round him to condole with him as well as provide domestic support. However, to help him overcome or numb his grief, Kizito applied for transfer out of his current station and was obliged. He was relocated abroad with his children.

After seven (7) years, he returned to the in-country headquarters of his company as Engineering Manager. He continued his holistic focus on his job and children – with zero hour for personal life. He admitted to his best friend, Frank, that he had not been with any woman since he became a widower. His parents were worried and pressured him to remarry, but he would not even consider the thought – until he met Adesuwa, who is about five years older than Kizito.

In Adesuwa, Kizito found a mother, sister, confidant and guardian. Adesuwa, a divorcee with two adult children from her first marriage is set on ensuring Kizito makes "commitment to holy matrimony". However, Kizito is emotionally unsettled and clearly conflicted. After two sessions with him, Kizito agreed to organize his emotional conflicts into a communication to *Emotionally Yours*. His letter provided the foundational basis for his internal conflict, which is currently affecting his work, relationship with his children and Adesuwa who is set on marrying Kizito.

Dear Emotionally Yours,
I want to thank you for your patience during our previous face-to-face discussion on my peculiar problem. Initially, I felt awkward, but was surprised by how you gently guided the discussions and made me discuss very painful episodes of my

life from a comic stance. I am really encouraged to table my conflicts to enable you analyze independently.

I will not repeat the painful circumstances that made me lose my first true love and the mother of my priceless jewels. When Veronica said she wanted children in quick succession to free her from secondary infertility possibilities, I was worried; little did I know that a Divine Hand was propelling it. Today, Vera 16, Kosi 14 and Michael 13, are my greatest joy and fulfillment. Vera is a 100% 'reincarnation' of Veronica – a High Definition Scan Version – only prettier due to innocence.

Since Veronica's death seven years ago, I have taken care of my children alone. How I have been able to cope with three teenagers is still baffling, but I give thanks to God. At 47 – approaching 48 years, I am very fulfilled. Incidentally, I have also come to the point where the children are focused on their education. I refused a Boarding School for them, as I need to come home and go over their assignments - as well monitoring their school challenges. My weekends are dedicated to mentoring and counseling them – and they look forward to weekends because I am able to give them quality time.

I met Adesuwa and fell in love with her maturity, knowledge and faith. Her commitment to church programs and non-for-profit organizations is inspiring. Her two sons (26 and 22 years old) display a high level of discipline. She is also admired and respected by her friends. Notwithstanding that she is five years older than me, she shows me respect. However, there are areas of slight disagreement and misalignment of

29

*thoughts that have kept me uneasy about moving to the next
level of expectation – marriage.*

*Adesuwa insists that OUR children could be an impedi-
ment to our happiness in marriage. There is no reasoning
with her on this matter as she states that she has 'brought up
two grown men' to know that my teenage children 'would be
in the way'. According to Adesuwa, we should "restart our
life without impediment of children." Incidentally, Adesuwa's
children have completed their university education, while
mine are in secondary school.*

*Another source of discomfort is her desire for us to relo-
cate to another city without work consideration. She wants
me to retire, get my benefits and join her in business, and
have enough time for each other – and have a baby of our
own. According to Adesuwa, she had a 'vision and revelation'
that the Company will soon collapse.*

*I love Adesuwa – not the way I loved my wife. Adesuwa
gives me a sense of security and peace. She is not beautiful in
the ways of the world, but she is charming and intelligent. I
get the chilly feeling whenever she talks about having "our
baby". Between Adesuwa and I there are five children – two
adults and three teenage children. Medically, at 54, she is
past childbearing age and at 47, I am not looking forward to
changing diapers and day care center regime. If we didn't
have children that consideration could have been logical.*

*I have lost count of how many times I tried to have mean-
ingful discussion on these issues with her, but every effort*

ends in a major disagreement and tempestuous quarrels. My family believes that I am' under some sought of influence'. My children are not comfortable with the relationship because Adesuwa seems set on 'ostracizing' me from my children. Vera, my 17 year old is very outspoken and threatened to run away. Vera is the split image of Veronica, my late wife. Unfortunately, Adesuwa has not done much to win the love of the children; she tells me that I ought to have trained my children to be emotionally independent – whatever that means.

*I love Adesuwa deeply and adore my children very much. I cannot imagine a life without my children. We have a bond/connection that is unimaginable. I am torn between love for my children and Adesuwa. **Is Adesuwa toying with my emotions by making impossible demands?**"*

At this time, Kizito's emotional problems have been impacting on his productivity at the company. His performance rating has gone down to below average – to the amazement of his Supervisor and Mentor. Also his relationship with his children, especially Vera, has gone frosty. Kizito's emotions stand on a TRIPOD – Work, Children and Adesuwa. The conflict is further deepened, as neither Adesuwa nor the children are ready to shift ground.

To understand the perspective of Kizito's children, an appointment was scheduled with Vera, the oldest of his children. An intelligent, smart but unassuming Vera posited:

"Madam Adesuwa is using foul powers to lure our father from his work and family. He is an excellent Engineer and

31

has several Excellence Awards to show – including one for 'Breakthrough Invention'. He is far from retirement and has no health challenges that could be given as the reason for retirement. I am about to start my university education later in the year. My brothers are still in secondary school; why would he consider retiring and relocating to some remote town. It is incredible that people can be that selfish…"

Furthermore, Vera stated they don't have good relationship with Adesuwa. "She is uppity and self-centered. Marrying my father will mean enslavement for us. I already told my grand parents (Maternal and Paternal), that the day my father legalizes his relationship with Madam Adesuwa, he ceases to be our father. He is all we have since Mom died. Our grandparents have told my father that Madam Adesuwa is evil and has an agenda that could cost his life. They have also been good to us, but no one can take over the role of your true parents. Our father has been the one taking care of us since Mom died over seven years ago.

"Did my father tell you that the her son tried to rape me in my own home? My brothers saved me from the beast. I reported the incident to my father, and, for the first time in my life, I didn't recognize him. Madam Adesuwa told him that I wore sexy lingerie to entice her son…Can you imagine that my father bought it – hook, line and sinker! You know what? Growing up, my mother forbade me from wearing nighties except pajamas (top and trouser). I have never worn any lingerie in my life. My father has lost it… I and my brothers are praying for him as marrying that woman will only spell doom for my brothers and I. Worst case scenario for me would be early marriage, but, what about my brothers? God is not sleeping. He will intervene…"

Discussions with Vera ended with an emotional note with *Emotionally Yours Team*. Everyone was moist and battling to hold the tears from coming down our cheeks. The battle for Kizito by Adesuwa has had an immeasurable emotional impact on his children, as they no longer speak to their father.

Emotionally Yours Program Counselor advised on the need to speak with Adesuwa. Adesuwa refused to meet with us; however, during the brief telephone discussion, I asked her "How do you plan to live with Kizito's children if you marry him eventually?" She quipped "Hell No. I am marrying the man with no baggage allowance on this trip. Bye."

Adesuwa's answer, taken at face value, confirmed Vera's fears that Adesuwa did not mean well. A barrage of questions coursed through my head: Why is Adesuwa doing this? Does she really love Kizito? Why is Adesuwa insensitive to the feelings of the children? Why is she not surrendering any grounds at all? Why is she bent of making the lives of these children an eternal misery.

Many Questions and postulations without answers…

It is pertinent to state that Adesuwa's response provided zero sentiments in responding to Kizito's emotionally torn mail on the problem. 'Love' sometimes can cause behavioural disharmony. 'Love' expressed by emotional twists and turn, hills and valleys and general disorientation. Whenever our emotional state begins to affect commonsensical reasoning, it becomes dangerous, and, sometimes, lethal. Many deadly mistakes have been made in defense of 'love' or emotions. The intertwined nature of 'love' and 'emotion' make some to blind-side the truth. *For, true love is RATIONAL and BEN-EFICIAL.*

Based on the foregoing, response to Kizito was crisp and straight to the point devoid of sentiments.

My Dear Kizito,
Your communication on above subject matter a month ago here refers.

Your emotional disposition at this time is unfortunate; clearly you are conflicted and dithering about where the pendulum should fitfully swing. The question that comes to mind is "Can true love evoke these negative emotions and conflicts?" The answer is clearly 'NO'. Therefore permit us to take components of this basket of confusion separately to enable you reach rational conclusion

Adesuwa. The woman at the center of your confusion is a successful, self-assured woman with a very independent spirit. She seems dictatorial in determining the structure of your relationship by 'directing' you retire from work, invest your gratuity into a joint business, run a joint account and send your children away – either Boarding Houses or 'abroad'. Your voice seems lost, as you did not raise a differing opinion.

34

True love is not designed to cause pain or confusion. True love causes harmony by gathering all discordant variables into a collective rhythm and dance. True love has inbuilt welding and sieving mechanism for the collective good. Your 'love' for Adesuwa seems far removed fr/ nom all elements of true love. It has brought you mental and emotional instability – having negative effect on your performance at work. It is also affecting the harmony you have enjoyed at home with your children.

If Adesuwa truly loves you, she will be sensitive to matters that affect you. She knows that you love your children; she knows that you cannot be at peace if you are suddenly separated from them. Above all, as a mother, she knows that the children are at the most critical stage of their emotional and mental development – they are teenagers. Anyone who loves you unconditionally will value the things or issues that will negatively affect you.

Adesuwa's 'love' for you is questionable. A love that leaves you an emotional wreck and crippled is not a recommended entanglement or liaison. You need to re-evaluate that 'feeling' and put it to test, using time tested values and variables - some of which have been earlier outline.

Adesuwa's Quest for Early Retirement. *Adesuwa made your early retirement one of the conditions for marrying you. From her perspective, your terminal benefits will be invested in her current business, expand her current 'profitable' business and have you as Executive Chairman. From our discussion, it was deduced that you are not 'inclined to doing* business'. *You have job satisfaction and fulfillment; therefore, do not desire to quit, especially, with company's children educational benefits included in your current remuneration. Again, though your performance appraisal is wanting, there is no threat to your job security.*

Kizito, it is clear that Adesuwa does not have your best interest at heart by suggesting early retirement – for the sole reason of expanding a business you know absolutely nothing about.

Furthermore, her plan for relocation to a new city is generally disturbing; a sentiment shared by you parents, close friends, associates and most importantly, your children. Clearly, Adesuwa's desire is to 'uproot' you from everyone you love because you have neither visited the intended location, nor have any friend or associate there. This kind of 'love' is very suspicious.

Kizito, please listen to your inner man.

Your children. *During our sessions, you described your children as your jewels. Jewels need to be cared for and appreciated. Vera was nearly raped under your roof by Adesuwa's son, Frank; rather than berate him, you believed Adesuwa's submission that your daughter was romantically enticing her son. Vera is hurt and does with Adesuwa who judged, rather than empathize with her. She also did not reproach her son, which is an indication that she is weak disciplining her children.*

It is evident that Adesuwa does not have a motherly instinct, as she has not made any efforts to initiate the process for harmonious living among the children (hers and yours).

Also, Adesuwa's plan to send your children to some 'far away institution' is very disturbing. There is nothing wrong with your children going to a Boarding School, but it becomes suspicious if it is condition precedent for your marriage. As a mother, she ought to know that teenage years are the most critical in a child's development. It can be deduced that Adesuwa's seeming dictatorial directive on the children is making them rebellious.

Kizito, your children love you very much, so, carefully think through issues concerning your children; make an effort to discuss with them in order to understand their perspective(s). A vacation alone with the children will provide the enabling environment for them to vent and table their charter of demands and needs with regard to Adesuwa and your good self.

We are optimistic that you will make the right decision…

Emotionally Yours

Five months later, an excited Kizito visited our office with a big thank you cake. According to Kizito, Adesuwa had insisted on being part of the vacation schedule. "I told her that I needed to spend some quality time with the children. Since Adesuwa came into my life, I suddenly realized that I didn't have time for my Vera, Kosi and Mike. Hell was let loose and

37

Adesuwa went berserk insisting she must come with us. Vera challenged her and during the heated exchange, Adesuwa said "My feet have been planted in this house and nothing, absolutely nothing, nobody can uproot me." I was taken aback because there was no competition for my heart. I am a straightforward man, and I don't believe in having multiple partners. She swore that she would make sure I lost my job if she is left behind. She was like someone deranged – a total stranger. I couldn't help but wonder what the problem was. I took the decision right there to get Adesuwa out of our lives for good. Oh, how she toyed with my emotions. She is very desperate. Men ought to be careful of such desperados."

During the trip, Kizito and the children met Antoinette, his late wife's friend who is now widowed. Vera and her brothers connected with Antoinette's two adorable teenage daughters, making the vacation fun-filled. Antoinette, a medical doctor was thrilled to meet with Veronica's children and bonded easily, telling them stories of their late mother.

Since their return, Antoinette and her daughters have been spending long hours and weekends with Kizito's family. Kizito says, "I am truly at peace. Antoinette is great with the children. She is a disciplinarian, but she also offers prices for good behaviour. She is firm and fair in her dealings with all the children. The future is in God's hands, but I am free..."

Emotional Piggy Bank

Love is the greatest gift from God. Without love, our lives would be colourless and meaningless. To love is to live and to connect physically, emotionally, mentally, spiritually and materially. Love means enduring the worst habit and helping your beloved navigate through a variety of painful emotions to overcome that bad habit. The joy that comes from triumphing over negative habits (hand-in-hand with the person you love) is overwhelming.

True Love gives life the Rainbow-Effect. However, it is important to understand HOW your 'love' evolves. True love influences behaviour positively, and it is rational and sensible. Blind? No! True love INFLUENCES and REINFORCES positive attitude in us. True love refines and modifies our behaviour and overall disposition to life's challenges with our partners. Thus, It is pertinent to keep emotions on the rational plane whenever conflicts arise. Conflicts help us to get the cobwebs of our emotions out and enables us experience the beauty of love in all its ramifications as enshrined in the Good Book – I Corinthians 13.

3

Episode 3

When Love Feels So Wrong
Marrying My Ex's Best Friend

My preferred timing for weddings is the cold season – including rainy season. I believe in the power of the weather; it is nothing empirical, but the weather has a coordinating influence. Choose a good weather for a wedding and I can conceptualize and mentally run you through a beautiful event. That is one of my Special Gifts.

Many people do not pay cognizance to Seasons when planning 'Holy Matrimony' events. Whenever you ask me why I prefer the cold season, my response is simple: "Cold Seasons are Peaceful and have a special effect on the ambience of the hall and mood of the people. Cold seasons make wedding ceremonies more somber – and spiritual. Vows are taken with unimaginable solemnity and candour. Each "I Do" comes through sincerely, while songs sound like 'covenants' by each attendee with God. Everyone looks to the couple with admiration because open declaration of love is a BRAVE Step. The next time you attend a 'Cold Season' event, you will agree with me.

This episode is not about weddings and weather conditions; it is not about taking vows solemnly, it is about the mental conflicts of when loving is 'right' or 'wrong'. Love is a positive phenomenon with an awesome feeling – sometimes light-headed and other times light footing.

For a human-interest reporter, the best of scoops can be picked up at wedding ceremonies. Early arrival and robed with the colours of the day readily grants you free access to 'restricted information' about the couple and family members. If you were gifted with a 'nose for news' and how to be a 'news hound' – with the appropriate familiar mannerism of a pretended 'insider', you would make your editors happy.

For a significant few, the need to probe hard for privileged family secrets is unnecessary. For, the best strategy is to dress the way you want to be addressed. My blessed mother taught me the importance of timeliness, and how to be distinguished – even when attired in 'hand me downs'. She also taught me the virtue of attending only occasions that sits right with my spirit man.

Mary-Jane (MJ) and Kelechi (Kels) were to be married during my favourite season. MJ's stepmother was excited about giving away her stepdaughter who had been a 'thorn on her flesh'. MJ is the daughter (and only child) of her husband's late wife and a constant reminder that her husband's first love was MJ's mother. Kels is a banker from a noble family – and deemed 'overdue' for marriage. His parents were excited that their son would finally settle down for good – but not happy with his choice. Kels has suffered many disappointments from ladies. They are doing what all parents do – support their son, despite their misgiving about the choice he has made. Kels was set to marry his ex-fiancée's best friend!

On arrival at the church, I observed the rows were scantily occupied, while there were clusters of groups whispering – some in consternation and others enjoying mocking laughter. The reporter's instinct whelmed within me. Dressed in the 'Family Colours', I walked to the rows dedicated for family members and sat confidently after exchanging pleasantries with others. Studiously, I read the program brochure, which was expensively printed. The lady to my right nudged me and asked, "Why do you people want to allow this marriage to take place? My grandson, Kels, is already engaged to this woman's best friend. Why? This generation…"

I was taken aback by her brazenness and unbridled negative demeanor; I smiled innocently to observe closely. After some introductions, I realized that the woman beside me is the grandmother to the groom. I was neither here for the bride or groom. The bride's stepmother is an acquaintance of my Auntie who 'ordered' me to attend on her behalf. A visibly worried Matriarch Eunice (Grandma) told me she was there to lay a curse on the 'witch' that wants to destroy her grandson. Kels is from a semi-priestly family and should live 'a righteous life'.

Grandma continued: "My grandson brought a well mannered and spiritually nurtured girl last December. Her name is Stella. She is from a solid Christian family. My family loved her very much and blessed the union at the village with every family member visiting home at the time. During the Easter celebrations, my grandson came home alone; we enquired about 'our wife'. He told us that he had a misunderstanding with Stella; I knew he was lying. I personally called Stella and she told me the truth about what happened. My grandson wanted her to get pregnant to fast track the wedding. My girl said, 'NO'. She wanted courtship according to true God's standards. That is all... The next thing I heard was that my grandson had set a date for wedding; behold it is Stella's friend. And you think God will bless this union? *Tufiaa...*" (Expression of an abomination)

Grandma Eunice continued this tiresome tirade that made my stomach churn. I looked around the church auditorium for escape opportunity; finding none, I latched unto the old trick that works all the time – 'need to use the bathroom'. Bathrooms have gossip milling machines. As anticipated, everything Grandma told me was being replayed in different varieties of colours and spices. Opinions differed based on re-

44

lational ties, while many were clearly neutral putting themselves in MJ's position. A dark cloud has been cast on the credibility of the ceremony.

I returned to my seat wondering what was delaying the commencement of the program. We were 90 minutes behind the scheduled 10:00 a.m. for the event. The church auditorium was half-filled with people; most of them had become very impatient and irritable. Grandma Eunice nudged me and said with a smirk: "I told you this union is cursed. My grandson has not come and the witch of a bride has been stood up for good." Almost simultaneously, the coordinating minister announced that the wedding program had been called off. Mixed reactions followed, and Grandma shouted, "Praise the Lord, Hallelujah" waltzing to the exit door.

Upset by the turn of events, I called my Auntie whom I had come to represent to update her on the turn of events. She was livid with rage as Kels is her godson. We hooked up later to visit with Kels to understand the reason for 'embarrassing MJ' at the altar. Kels had locked himself in his room, terrified by shame and gossips arising from the incident. After minutes of persuasion, he opened the door for my Auntie, who held me closely like a clutch bag. Without any preamble, my Auntie asked: "Kels, what is the matter? I am not here to berate you. I am happy that you took this stand … Marriage is an Everlasting Covenant. So, honey, tell me what the problem is…"

Kels looked up and our eyes locked; I could see a visibly embarrassed young man – very ashamed of his cowardly act.

Auntie reassured him that I was there to help him through the forest of emotional turmoil. Trust my Auntie to put me in a situation like this without prior briefing! Seeing him relax a little, I asked him pointedly: "So, tell us, why did you do it, Kels?" He asked for a shot of whisky; my auntie reached out and handed him half a glass, despite my weak protests. Thankfully, Kelechi took a sip, discarded the drink, and spoke almost in a soliloquy...

"Can love be wrong?" he muttered as he opened up.
"My problem is all because of my EX-Fiancée. Stella is a very enterprising and Godly young woman. We dated for about two years. From the moment we met, I knew this was the one I had waited for. She helped me curb my life of excesses and extravagance, and taught me financial planning - how to committedly save. As a banker, I should be the one giving her stringent controls on money matters. Stella is nothing like any of the young ladies I dated in the past. She does not pay attention to jewelry and expensive clothing. She believes in functionality and would always advise on the need to invest rather than consume.

"Months back, in my desperation to make her mine at all cost, I suggested that she could get pregnant because her parents had reservations about me. She strongly disagreed with me and stressed the need for Christian courtship. I sometimes even accused her of pretending and double dating because I thought that she was 'too pious'. Unknown to her, her best friend MJ actually wanted her out of the way. MJ, who works as a Hospitality Officer in one of the big hotels, is at least three years older than Stella - and desperately desirous of settling down. She planted seeds of doubt in my heart and I gradually created a gulf between us and became very apprehensive of the relationship. MJ visited frequently without Stella during this period. My younger sister openly challenged MJ on her frequent visits and long stay at my residence. MJ lied that Stella asked her to visit me to help mend the fragile relationship. Gradually, things went out of control and she became pregnant.

"My Grandmother was distraught about the development because Stella had stolen her heart – including every member of the family. My parents were very disappointed in me, but could not suggest abortion. However, MJ's stepmother insisted that I should marry MJ, who is older than me. Can you imagine? Mum and dad bowed to pressure because of their positions in the church. Unfortunately, my courage failed me as I could not go through with the wedding. How can I marry my fiancée's best friend? This cannot be 'love', and if it is, then it is wrong. This love feels wrong. Why do I feel so much burden of guilt?

"MJ confesses she loves me very much, but I have doubts. With the benefit of hindsight, I think that she orchestrated everything in their sequence. She started by dropping the poison of doubt about Stella's sincerity. She criticized Stella whenever we had the opportunity to be alone. Each time I look at her, I see past her, with Stella towering above her. I have had nightmares; I have gone for confessions – including deliverance. MJ concluded that Stella bewitched me, but I know it is my conscience that is restless because the poor girl did nothing wrong in putting her feet down that she would not use pregnancy as the shortcut to making her parents accept me. Stella believed that with patience and prayers, her parents would accept me eventually. Stella's parents said I am a playboy who would hurt their daughter…. See how right they are?

"Now, MJ is pregnant for me – according to her. I feel I need to settle my emotional confusion first. I am not sure about what I feel for her – love or lust. My dad said that marriage is NOT about sex; honestly, that is what I think MJ and I have. No marriage can be sustained by something as pedestrian as sex. I know I am a coward for not coming to church or facing MJ to tell her this charade cannot continue. But, I cannot raise my child in this arena of falsehood. I have succeeded in tying a noose around my neck. I need to deal with it….

"You know, sometimes I feel like I am being manipulated by MJ. Please tell me, is there a wrong time to love? How can you even tell when love is wrong? Love is supposed to be peaceful and fulfilling - that is what I felt with Stella. Do you think it is too late to return to Stella?"

Venting is good for emotional release. Kels had bottled so much during the course of his five-month-old relationship with Mary-Jane. He could neither speak with his parents nor siblings about his problems, while MJ mounted undue pressure on him. The 'sudden pregnancy' is another source of stress for Kels, thus, a rather subdued and confused Auntie turned to me with an 'Executive Order': "You need to find a way to fix Kels." What my auntie didn't know was that Kels was already 'fixing' himself up.

WHEN LOVE FEELS VERY WRONG

The most important step in resolving emotional confusion is going back to the root cause, establishing the enabling circumstances, and, identifying the variables that contributed to the situation. It is similar to walking back from the point of convergence to the solitary track. Emotional maturity is very critical in establishing the root cause when faced with a crisis situation like the one Kels found himself.

While many may consider it a weak disposition, sometimes, the most important step to take is "DO NOTHING". Proceeding with the wedding program could have driven a deeply emotionally unstable and depressed Kels into a state of near dementia. He was carrying emotional burdens of **Guilt, Regret, Denial and Betrayal** put together. The cocktail of negative expressions encapsulated him and made him a prisoner to his mistakes. He had no clarity of purpose in accepting the 'love' dished out to him by Mary-Jane. He *vengefully* wanted to 'show' Stella that she could easily be replaced; incidentally, he fell into the warm embrace of a 'bride in waiting'.

Further interactions with Kels revealed that, "MJ always felt that Stella overshadowed her. Many within their circle of friends always identified her as 'Stella's friend', and she hated that." Kels' friends, Somto and Michael had major disagreements with him over his 'choice of love'. They tried to dissuade him from his chosen path, but no one can direct the heart how to love and who to love. With the current complications, his friends left him alone to bear the consequences of his action of 'loving wrongly'.

Three weeks after the botched wedding, defying the heavy June downpour, I visited Kels' home to know how he was healing from the emotional crisis. In the company of his friends, Kels seemed more self-assured. His mother had just called everyone to the dining table for lunch when a visibly pregnant MJ walked in. She was sobbing, walking straight to where Kels was sitting: "Why are you doing this to me? Is it wrong to fall in love with you? Do you want us to have our first child out of wedlock? Why, Kelechi, Why?"

To the consternation of everyone, Kels remained very calm all through MJ's hysteria. Kels displayed unrivalled maturity and confidence - a very distant image from the young man who was suicidal about a month ago. Kels took MJ in his arms and guided her to a comfortable sofa, while asking his mother to prepare MJ a glass of fresh fruit juice. Time ceased as the silence in the living room could make the sound of a pin echo like a thunderbolt. Kels reached out for the glass and handed over to MJ, requesting her to relax. Truly, time is a very effective balm.

We all held our breath as Kels spoke in a tone depicting finality and judgment. "Mary-Jane, please listen to me. We have made mistakes, and I hold myself totally responsible for everything that happened. We will be deluding ourselves if we think this is true love. This is fleshly desire called 'lust' because we were feeding our biological needs. I was sex-starved in my previous relationship and embraced your affection. It is not fair, but it is now clear to me that I was on a rebound. I am sorry about everything, but our child will be provided for. If it is the Will of God that we will marry, nothing will stop it. Please, MJ, let us step out of the current situation and focus on our innocent child. Let us build on the friendship we have and see what the future holds for us. These last couple of weeks has been hell; I am trying to put the pieces of this puzzle together without success. Please bear with me…"

Kels shocked everyone, including his parents. Mary-Jane cried uncontrollably. There were mixed emotions as she muttered repeatedly, "I should have known…Oh, my God…" Kels' mother walked towards MJ, signaled me as she pulled her into her arms and guided her to the guest room, assuring her that all would be well. At this time, only a mother's love can cushion the impact of the scenario that played out earlier.

As she continued to cry, Mary-Jane could not but come to terms with the fact that sometimes our emotions can be deceptive. The intensity of the emotion does not translate to 'love'. True love is nurtured and constantly weighted. Is there a time love can be wrong? Clearly, the answer is NO; however, the thin line between love and lust can be confusing. While feeding on fleshly need, lust has the intensity capable of confusing even the most experienced relationship experts.

Emotional Piggy Bank
The greatest emotional baggage to any relationship is getting involved with your best friend's ex fiancé/fiancée. To be successful under such circumstances, deception and lies must be ruled out and placed on a pedestal of transparency.

Emotions and feelings need to be constantly weighted when taking actions that would possibly impact one's future or that of an innocent child. True love can occur at any time. It does not have time limitations or hurtful. True love is never wrong, rather it is rewarding, as it is also responsive and responsible. Nevertheless, players must ensure that they understand the context of every emotional depth in order to apply required checks and protect the heart from heartbreak.

We need to constantly put a strong lien on our emotions after a separation or divorce. Unchecked emotions may inadvertently lead one to a rebound effect. Some rebounds can be more hurtful than the actual separation. Let us continue to be mindful of Wise King Solomon's recommendation: "Keep your heart with all diligence; for out of it springs the issues of life". Proverbs 4:23

4

Episode 4

The God-Factor in Emotional Conflicts
Raped and Impregnated By Armed Robbers

The mystery involved in making children is beyond human comprehension. Man's infinite dimensions cannot measure it, no matter how gifted you are. It has become a universal principle that every family yearns to have numeric increment via natural procreative process. Those not inclined to have children due to personal preferences opt for child adoption in line with approved processes.

While Science attempts to describe the egg fertilization

through to eventual birthing processes, there are limitations in explaining HOW the mix of spermatozoon and egg co-join and how the liquid dropped for fertilization. Conversely, Science has not conclusively explained how infertility sets in and the true state of the internal system of the woman. I love how Dr. Randy J. Guliuzza's submission in *"Made in His Image: Human Reproduction"* to Institute for Creation Research:

"Actually, the detail could go far beyond this simple description. As seen, the level of coordinated interaction to get any viable offspring exceeds the cellular level, extends past the reproductive system, pulls in the neurologic, hormonal, and circulatory systems, and demands substances that are produced independently by the male to modify the actions of the female body or the materials made by her--and vice versa. Evolutionary literature is rife with speculative stories about the origination of these processes, but devoid of any real scientific evidence to explain them. The only viable explanation is that GOD placed these processes in the first parents, Adam and Eve, fully functional right from the beginning."

Truly, bringing forth a child into the world is indeed an awesome experience!

Within the last five years, two very challenging emotional conflicts situations revolved around "accidental procreation". I want to operationally define accidental procreation circumstances as "birthing children as a result of forceful entry leading to pregnancy". The need for this definition is because some women have had to deal with pregnancies resulting from birth control mechanisms failure.

What would you do as a Pastor if armed robber invaded your December 31st Cross-Over Service and in the process raped your daughter? What would you do if you find out two months on, that your daughter is pregnant? How can a Pastor's daughter overcome the pain and shame of being violated, and, pregnant for an unknown criminal? How would she cope to full term? How would the Pastor and his wife explain their daughter's pregnancy out of wedlock? Would the Pastor and his wife accept their first 'grandchild' as a blessing? What is the way out? Many unanswered questions!

Again, what would you do if after 19 years of 'searching for the fruit of the womb', hoodlums invaded your home, gang-raped you. Four months down the line, you realize that the gang rape experience resulted in multiple pregnancy – triplet? What would a loving husband do under this circumstance? Would this couple welcome these 'innocent children' as 'Divine Intervention? How would the man react under this trying situation?

After over 10 years of working emotional cases, one lesson that reverberates is the fact that primary colours do not define emotional conflicts and entanglements. There are underlying and extenuating circumstances, enveloped by actions and reactions. These realities challenge the Emotional Counselor beyond rationality and simple logic. Incidents sometimes challenge fundamental beliefs and mores. Thus, the best counsel is offered from a painful impassioned pedestal, having identified variables holistically and individualistically.

Negative emotions must be extricated and flushed for the delivery of, sometimes, painful path towards emotional crisis resolution. These two unfortunate incidents, at some stage led to victims' doubt of the Omnipotent, Omniscient and Eternal God Factor! However, the story of the Okes is very significant because of its emotional complexities.

Twenty-two year old Sandra was a Year 2 Bio-Medical Sciences student of a reputable institution. On December 23, she returned home for the Christmas holiday season full of expectations and plans. Her father, Pastor Oke is a well-known and respected preacher, who lives and walks the Word, bringing his children up in alignment with the Word of God. Pastor Oke's children were love by neighbours and church members for their cultured manner. Mrs. Oke is a paragon of beauty and humility; she runs a foundation that caters for the girl child. In addition to supporting her husband, Mrs. Oke runs one of the cheapest Nursery/Primary Schools in the State.

The Okes look forward to December 31st every year with excitement and expectations – new resolutions, family plans and programs for the following year and a host of wish lists. The most important part of the period was the opportunity for January 1st Family Feedback Hour, when family members provide feedback Mom and Dad on parenting style. For Sandra, she always enjoyed the opportunity to tell her parents things she did not like and what her parents needed to refrain from doing 'going forward'. So, coming home every December was not negotiable, because it was critical for family bonding.

The Okes had a great day – last minute year-end shopping and general preparation for the New Year. There was an air of spirituality amid sober reflection of the ending year. After dinner, they drove to the hired venue of the Cross-Over Service, an open area less than 10 minutes drive from their residence. A cheery congregation welcomed Pastor Oke and his family; as they step in, the environment electrified with praise and worship. It was an excited Minister that stepped up to the podium at precisely 2330hrs to commence the Crossover and Testimony Night program.

Thirty minutes into the Praise and Adoration, the "Happy New Year" was announced amid shouts of exultation and adoration. Fireworks outside the service environment added to the already electrified worship center as the congregation danced to 'sow into the new year'. Then the unexpected happened, as armed men in masks, who ordered every worshipper to lie flat on their face, surrounded Pastor Oke at the podium. They made away with the collections, and dispossessed the congregation of their valuables. The gang also escorted some members identified as 'wealthy' out into their vehicles. At the protest of the Pastor, the four men descended on him, beating him to a stupor.

Sandra could no longer lie still. She got up to fight one of the hoodlums in defense of her father. Sandra's martial arts training came handy as he rescued her dad from the villain. Unfortunately, two of the gang pinned her to the ground, beat her up really bad; it was under this tensed circumstance that the leader of the gang tore off her clothes and decided to 'teach her the lesson of her life'. He violated her mercilessly to the point of losing consciousness. It was the longest nightmare of her life as Sandra floated between the pain of being raped and violently beaten.

Time stood still as Sandra and her father regained consciousness at the private hospital of a church member, her father's bosom friend of many years, Dr. Umez, who had called for his hospital's Ambulance. Pastor Oke was in pains when he came to, asked after his family, to which the doctor professionally responded: "everyone is fine". Mrs. Oke did not leave her daughter's side, and appealed to the doctor and key staff to maintain professional confidentiality by not telling her husband that Sandra was raped and severely beaten. Dr. Umez ordered several tests and treatments for Sandra; all members of the medical team worked frantically to ensure that all was well with Sandra and her father.

Mrs. Oke was treated for shock because witnessing her daughter violated and husband almost killed, was too much to bear. However, she managed to appeal for utmost confidentiality in matters regarding Sandra. After two weeks of hospitalization, father and daughter were discharged to the joy of the family and Pastor Oke's congregation, many of whom were not very sure of 'what really happened to Sandra'.

Through the efforts of a 'protective mother' who was guarding against stigmatization, there were conflicting stories concerning the incident. Some believed that Sandra was beaten to a pulp for "trying to be heroic"; others were sure that she was "attempting to call the Police" while another group said Sandra was "taking pictures of the invaders". Yet, another group were convinced that Sandra "recognized some members of the gang" hence, the 'serious beating' she got. However, everyone empathized with her and thanked God for making sure 'no life was lost'.

Sandra returned to school with the trauma as all rape victims, and thrust herself into the academic workload to distract her from the nightmares she experienced. She became a hermit and made conscious efforts to avoid male classmates. Efforts by close friends who knew she was 'beaten by invading robbers' paled into insignificance as Sandra rebuffed entreaties for group studies and campus fellowships.

Early February, Sandra fainted during a lecture session; her best friend, Pamela called Mrs. Oke who flew down to see her daughter at the university clinic. She immediately arranged for her transfer to Dr. Umez's private hospital, the family hospital. Different tests were conducted: HIV/AIDS, Pneumonia, Diabetes, Malaria, Typhoid, Pap smear, Appendicitis, Low sugar, PCV, etc. Nothing significant was found.

After one week of hospitalization, Dr. Umez, Medical Director decided to indulge his 'whim'; he took a blood sample to three outside laboratories for pregnancy test. Results came back positive. He was devastated, asking himself repeatedly: How would he tell Sandra's mother that the real nightmare had begun? How would he face Pastor Oke, his dear friend of many years, to explain that Sandra was raped the same night he (Pastor) nearly died in the hands of the violent gang – resulting in pregnancy? How do you tell this to a mother who is yet to recover from the trauma of witnessing her daughter raped and husband beaten close to death?

Finally, he decided that there was no time to waste; Mrs. Oke needed to the situation to enable to family decide on what to do. Adopting reverse psychology, Mrs. Oke was asked what she honestly thought could be wrong with her daughter. She suggested it could be depression and fear that people knew she was raped. Dr. Umez reminded her that the personnel with the highest level of integrity coordinated post-rape treatment for Sandra. At the suggestion that Pregnancy Test would be done the next day, Mrs. Oke went berserk: "No. No. No. Don't even think or suggest that Sandra could be pregnant. Do you know what that means? My husband's Ministry will be finished! Have you considered what a pregnancy will mean to my daughter? Please perish the thought…"

Moved with compassion, Dr. Umez prayed for Divine Wisdom on how to communicate the 'bad news', fully aware that it was more dangerous to delay the information further. He needed to alter the Sarah's medications to pregnancy-friendly ones decision on the pregnancy, but decided to update Pastor Oke on the situation to get a steer on the matter. Unaware of the pregnancy, but knew that it was expedient that her husband knew about the rape. At last, the secret of those fateful early hours of January 1 was going to be revealed. Would her husband feel disappointed and betrayed in her? Would he ever trust her again? How will Sandra feel IF the test proved positive…. Many disturbing questions…

Pastor agreed to create time Sunday evening to meet with his friend and chat over dinner. Ahead of the dinner meeting, Pastor Oke and his wife checked on their daughter, Pastor insisting that Sarah needed deliverance since nothing is medically wrong with her. Dr. Umez was glad to see his friend in high spirit, wondering how the day would end after delivering the sad message. He hated being the harbinger of bad news, and, it was the first time they were meeting socially, besides church services, since the unfortunate incident.

They had dinner in silence amid palpable tension; Dr. Umez ate mechanically, his mind pre-occupied, mentally joggling one possible strategy after the other. Walking with Pastor Oke and his wife in tow to the study, he knew that the die was cast and silently prayed for divine strength. "I want to begin with apologies. I have failed you as a friend and failed God as His child..." he began. A surprised Pastor Oke looked to his wife who sat with head bowed, believing Dr. Umez was about to reveal Sarah's ordeal that fateful night.

"As you know, Sandra has been in the hospital for about two weeks...I just found out that she is pregnant..." Dr. Umez dropped the bombshell. Pastor Oke gave his wife a questioning look, "What...what did you just say? Sandra, my daughter is pregnant? How?" Turning to his wife, "Is this true? Are you aware of this? Speak, woman..." Dr. Umez interrupted, "My brother, mummy does not know that she is pregnant; that is why I decided to come to the house. We did not tell you everything about that night.... Those hoodlums raped Sandra, our dear daughter. Unfortunately, it has resulted in a pregnancy. I thought it wise to discuss with both of you.

Something needs to be done, and, fast too…. My apologies Mummy; this burden has been too much for me…" he concluded with visible relief.

Mrs. Oke wept uncontrollably, while her husband stared unseeingly and motionless. When he spoke, it was to no one; he soliloquized: "Lord, what is my crime? Who has sinned in this family? What are you trying to tell me, Lord? Have I not served you faithfully? Are you visiting our sins on my beloved daughter? What kind of shame is this, Lord…?" Dr. Umez quietly left to the home of the Okes, making a mental note to return first thing the next morning. There are key issues that need to be resolved and the earlier the better.

For the Okes, it was the longest night of their lives. Painfully, Mrs. Oke narrated what took place that fateful night and how everything was done to clean up and treat their traumatized daughter who was violently raped. She pleaded with her husband to persuade Dr. Umez not to disclose to Sandra that she was with child – and to secretly abort the baby. Pastor Oke was indeed in dire straits – he could neither pray nor reason with his wife. He lamented all night.

Dr. Umez had invited me earlier to provide my perspective – a 'third eye' angle, but I dithered. He got to his friends' residence the next morning only to discover that they never left the study. Husband and wife sat down in deep thought with confused expressions. Dr. Umez was concerned and checked their blood pressures; the results were so alarming that he gave them medication to relax them. He left with instructions to the housekeeper that the couple should neither be disturbed nor allowed to receive any visitors. He knew his friends would need their strength to deal with the issue at hand. Sandra had been requesting for a private session with the doctor to understand her 'ailment'.

The meeting with Sandra's parents was one of the most emotionally tense sessions I have ever dealt with. Discussions focused on "How to manage the information"; "Is abortion the answer?" "How will the church perceive their Pastor in view of the Sandra's pregnancy? "Would the Pastor approve abortion as a necessity under the circumstance?" "Will Pastor accept that his first grandchild is seared by a criminal?" So many questions…

This couple was crestfallen. They needed a shock treatment that would kick-start them back to reality. I empathized with the Pastor Oke, who is one of the few 'true men of God' with the highest level of ethics and integrity I have met. He was loved for his stance on Christian discipline, piety and morality. Clearly, in this circumstance, Pastor Oke and his daughter, Sandra, are most impacted. Aware that they had not had anything to eat in almost 24 hours, Dr. Umez called on the housekeeper to get some green tea and freshly made juice, for it was going to be a long evening. Introductions and exchanges were made while waiting for refreshment.

We took refreshment in silence, but the tension was palpable as Dr. Umez gave me a nudge. One of the most trying periods for even the most experienced and talented professional is rationally surfing through entanglements. The need to explain real situations and their implications is usually a tough call. Dr. Umez and I had worked through the issues – all night and day – till the point of meeting - until he, too became very emotional.

Rationality is often impacted by uncoordinated feelings; this happens to be best of us, no matter your profession or vocation- including yours truly. "Pastor, I understand how you feel right now, but I believe that a prayer to kick off discussions will be good…. Please, lead us in a short prayer". That was an unkind cut, but it had to be done; it was the beginning the process of venting and healing for the family whose trust is in God. Initially, Pastor Oke looked at me with an inexplicable emotion, shaking his head, he knelt down and said a very short, but powerful prayer under the circumstance. His prayer cleared the path to emotional recovery: "*Lord Jesus, I thank you for everything; please, grant me the Grace to bear this great burden. Amen*"

That simple but powerful prayer changed the mood in the room. There seemed to be an entrance of Power that encapsulated the room with PEACE. Internal peace aids positive reasoning, and we needed a surplus dose of that for the discussion. Also, the wordings and tone of the prayer was a signal that everyone in the room was ready to accept the worst-case scenario. Above all, I was strengthened and more confident to deliver painful but critical perspective to the 'issues' at hand. It was brief, without sentiments and straight to the point:

"Thank you for allowing me to participate in this very intimate family matter. I am glad that we are all positively disposed to deal with the fact of the tough problem before us. This family is a high profile and well-respected family, and Pastor Oke is a revered minister of the Word. Therefore, we need to carefully consider the situation and take decisions towards remediation. We need to consider that Sandra is an adult who must be carried along in this matter that affects her directly. Yes, the situation if not well articulated and handled, will impact the family's reputation, Ministry, and most importantly, Sandra.

"While the seemingly easiest option is 'quiet abortion', Dr. Umez knows that he cannot wheel Sandra to the theatre without an explanation. She already suspects that she might be pregnant and has requested for a pregnancy test. When Dr. Umez and I playfully asked her what she would do if she were pregnant, Sandra shook her head and faced the wall. That is denial! The clock is ticking; the damage has been done, and I think we might consider the following steps:
1. ZERO consideration for Abortion
2. Relocate Sandra outside the country (preferably, the United States of America or United Kingdom) to have the baby and continue her education there
3. When the baby comes, send the baby to a Motherless Baby Home for possible adoption; OR, return the baby 'home' and be adopted into the Oke Family."

"No way", Mrs. Oke shouted. How can my first grandchild be a bastard, and, a product of rape? God forbid. Please Dr. Umez take out that thing…that bastard…. Oh God, why? Why? Why me? What did we do to deserve this? Who did we offend…."she sobbed uncontrollably. Her husband moved over to her side and held her tightly muttering "It is well; it is well; it will end in praise. Like Job, we will triumph. What else can we do? Abortion is against the Will of God. The shame is unimaginable, but I think they have thought this out well. It is a temporary option until things cool down. Please, my darling. Be strong..."

Pastor Oke decided to go with us to the hospital to see her daughter immediately. It was an apprehensive and confused Sandra who greeted us. Mrs. Oke wore a very sad and depressing countenance that increased Sandra's anxiety, "Daddy, Mummy, what is the problem? Is everything okay? Am I dying?" Pastor Oke moved to the bed, reassuring his daughter that "All is well", however, he had 'unfortunate news' to tell her. Sandra became hysterical: "Did I contact HIV/AIDS from the rape? Is it cancer? Oh, please, Mummy, tell me that I am not dying. I have seen the way the some of staff have been looking at me with so much pity...like I have limited days to live...Can someone tell me what I am suffering from..."

"God is Faithful; He is Merciful and Gracious. You do not have any 'Egyptian Disease'. We thank God for that; but you are pregnant..." Pastor Oke dropped the bomb! Minutes that seemed like an eternity passed, with a now uncontrollably hysterical Sandra pulled away from her father, tore off the drip and attempted to run away from the room without success. Dr. Umez tried to calm her down, overcoming his desire to sedate her. When she became calm, Sandra asked her mother, "Mummy, what am I going to do? How will I be able to face my friends in school and the church? Oh, Daddy, how will your members look at you – a minister whose daughter is pregnant out of wedlock…made pregnant by an armed robber? What kind of destiny is this…?" Sandra went on and on… Mrs. Oke held her daughter tight and the two women wept in tensed confusion.

One week later, the family adopted the *"Emotionally Yours Model"*, as Pastor Oke christened the advice provided that evening of crisis. Sandra spent some time with the *Emotionally Yours* Team to enable her vent and come to terms with the challenges of 'accidental motherhood', as she called it. Within three weeks, *Emotionally Yours Team* worked with its international network to get a Christian couple in Europe where Sandra was to live, school and have her baby – all with the support of her parents.

Emotional Piggy Bank

Rape victims experience emotional and psychological consequences beyond the constantly harped 'stigmatization'. Being raped by a criminal with the resultant consequence of pregnancy introduces another dimension in emotional distress. While victims fall back to self-blame as 'avoidance tool', 'spiritualizing' the incident further impacts the healing process. Post-traumatic stress disorder (PTSD), depression, flashbacks, sleep and disorders, guilt, anger and suicidal inclinations are recurring emotional pools in which victims swim.

Love, patience and understanding help victims rebuild their self-confidence, while crawling gradually from the stupor of depression through the rungs of self-awareness. It is Love's influence via expression of positive emotion and rational behaviour that help victims overcome, as well as come to terms with any other fall outs impacting on other parties. The constant reference to the word 'bastard' during pregnancy arising from a rape incident naturally reopens the wounds to a never-healing state. The incident is mentally relived and the cycle could be unending.

Therefore, Love is the BALM that soothes emotionally traumatized victim. Thus, the next time you meet a rape victim, show empathy, understanding and LOVE.

5

Episode 5

Emotional Triangle and Conflict
Can My Sons Revive My Husband's Love for Me?

Rabbi Edwin Friedman's work, **Generation to Generation: Family Process and Synagogue** focused on the application of the laws of emotional triangles. Dr. Thomas M. Smith detailed expression provide deeper insight and clarity to the concept, viz.: "These 'laws' govern the way all relationships work - they are embedded in the human personality and function accurately across cultures and ethnic groups. The basic premise is that two people tend to be unstable unless they are perfectly aligned in understanding and competent in honest communication. When one or the other becomes frightened or anxious in their two person relationship there is a strong desire to involve someone or something else - to make an alliance with someone or something - to buff up a position, to increase a sense of security in the context of conflict with the other person in the two person dyad ('group' of two people).

"So, the basic law is that when any two parts of a system become uncomfortable with one another they will 'triangle in' (focus upon) a third person, or issue, as a way of stabilizing their own relationship with one another. A person may be said to be 'triangled' if he or she gets caught in the middle as the focus of such an unresolved issue. Conversely, (and importantly), when individuals try to change the relationship of two others (two people, or a person and his or her symptom or belief), they 'triangle' themselves into that relationship (and often stabilize the very relationship they are trying to change).

"Typical emotional triangles found in families are mother-father-child; a parent and any two children; a parent, his or her child, and his or her parents; a parent, a child, and a symptom in the child (doing badly in school, drugs, stealing, sexual acting out, a medical condition); one spouse, the other spouse, and the other's dysfunction (drinking, gambling, an affair, a sexual addiction, depression). As you can readily see, the third part of a triangle isn't always a person -- it can be 'the bottle' or some other form of addiction, or even work or a hobby.

"Emotional triangles have very specific rules that they invariably obey. Awareness of these rules is immensely helpful in understanding the emotional processes swirling around us, and is helpful in allowing us to remain more objective about intense situations. As with all systems thinking, the concept of emotional triangles allows us to focus on process rather than content. In addition, it provides a new way to hear people, as well as criteria for what information is important."

In many cases, particularly in our clime, the basis of emotional triangle is often debased or seemingly nonsensical because the one who is arching towards the triangle, or the third party being 'triangled' are unaware of the depth of their actions or inactions. Children have been 'triangled' into many emotional crises unknowingly, which have had negative impacts on their relationships as adults. Women have been known to inadvertently use their children as emotional shields leading to early involvement in 'family emotional dramas'. Often, the frequency of these dramas impairs them emotionally. This partly explains why some husbands are seem 'cold' and 'insensitive', while a good number of wives are known to be 'frigid' or 'stone-cold'. These 'epithets' are attempts to explain how innocent and unwilling emotional triangle participants can be affected in later years because early experiences (good or bad) leave impressionable mark on individual emotional development and maturity.

This episode is not intended to be a lecture on emotional triangle; however, the introduction provides the foundational basis for appreciating the complexities of emotional issues in the lives of people close to us. It is important to realize that every mishandled relationship has the potential to lead players into emotional crisis; only those with understanding and emotional maturity survive. Sometimes, the best emotional preparation will not suffice because nobody enters a relationship looking forward to a time of emotional somersault. That was the case with Uduak and Ifiok who stayed married for 21 years despite environmental and economic challenges. The harsh economic situation was further compounded by two decades without a child.

Secondary School sweethearts, Uduak and Idiok jointly attended one of the prestigious universities in South-South region, Nigeria. After National Youth Service, they immediately gained employment in the oil and gas sector and wedded six months after. Idiok showcased Uduak as an epitome of godly lifestyle because she remained a virgin until their wedding night. Despite pressures from bosses and the wealthy around her, beautiful and elegant Uduak stayed faithful to her marriage vows. However, the couple continued to have skirmishes arising from Uduak's inability to be pregnant; there was no medical reason for Uduak's 'infertility".

During the 20th wedding anniversary, Ifiok's mother visited the couple, and gave Uduak a marching order to leave her son's house "for wasting 20 years of Idiok's life." Her husband resisted his mother's moves to get him another wife but failed, as his mother moved into his home with a young 'wife' to the painful embarrassment of Uduak. After two weeks of pressure from his mother, who applied all sentiments and blackmail to perfect her plans, Idiok gave in and accepted Rose as his second wife. Naturally, Uduak felt betrayed and protested her husband's action. Her mother in-law later connived with Rose to relocate Uduak to the Guest Room – without a contrary word from her husband. When Uduak later confronted her Idiok, she got nothing assuring, hence, she sought the advise of her mother. A pained and visibly worried mother advised her daughter to 'endure', but be prayerful.

Subsequently, Uduak submitted to fasting and praying because Rose took over the kitchen, refusing to give her food. Uduak became focused on her job; her rating at the office improved; she became married to her career. She developed a new routine in order to avoid depression or sinking into self-pity and paid more attention to her fashion and general appearance – loving things she gave up because of Idiok. Furthermore, she took short professional courses during the weekend to fill in the void at home. Uduak became a total stranger to her husband; everything she worked for had been taken over by the younger wife, Rose.

The greatest shock for Uduak was when she was also 'forbidden' from driving the car she bought with Company loan; Idiok gave the car to Rose. Her pain was aggravated due to exposure to the rains, but was fortunate to find a female junior colleague who lived a bus stop away from her house. Uduak humbly accepted riding with her to and from the office. However, Uduak preferred boarding public transport to avoid explaining to her situation at home to anyone. Nevertheless, it was an observant Supervisor that saw through the 'cosmetic smiles' to establish that all was not well with Uduak's marriage, but Mr. Lewis restrained himself from asking questions that may bother on impropriety.

Months later, her Department was subjected to Annual Business Reviews and Audit; Uduak spent long hour preparing, and later working with the External Auditors in her role as the Departmental Audit Contact. One fateful day, she worked till about 2200 hours – the latest in her work life. Although she felt uncomfortable working that late, Uduak knew that she was better off keeping her mind busy with work than going home to deal with Rose's antics and the cold attitude of her husband. The agonizing thought of her home fueled her adrenalin to complete the day's task and determined to commence the next day's schedules. Happy with her work accomplishment, Uduak called for the pre-approved company secure transportation to take her home. She eventually got home at 2245hours to meet an angry Idiok who plummeted her with slaps and blows calling her a 'corporate prostitute' and other unprintable names. After the physical abuse, she was assisted by one of the domestic staff to the guest room that had become her sanctuary these past months. While taking a warm shower, Uduak cried to God to take her life than live in this garden of sadness.

Surprisingly, she found herself praying for her husband, Idiok under the warm water, "Please Father forgive him, because I am to blame. He is angry because he has no child. God, you know everything. Please make Rose pregnant so that my husband's frustration can be over." Uduak was about sleeping when an angry husband came into her room and forced her to make love; Uduak resisted, directing him to his 'beautiful wife upstairs'. Idiok succeeded in 'violently raping' his wife. Uduak was so sore she could not go to work the next day and had to call in sick. The family doctor visited and gave her some medications, urging her to rest.

Two months later, on a bright and sunny Saturday morning, Idiok and his other wife, Rose, threw Uduak out of her home – with her personal effects scattered on the street for all to see. Jointly beating her, Rose called her a witch who was responsible for her many miscarriages since she married Idiok. Uduak was also accused of keeping an evil pot that had been draining Idiok's fortune; Idiok had been sacked for corruption from his place of work. Above all, she was also accused of having a spirit husband that was responsible for her inability to get pregnant. The residents were shocked by the development, but could not intervene, especially, when Uduak said nothing in her defense to all the accusations. She only repeatedly muttered, "My God, You are seeing... You are hearing..."

In her distress, Uduak made frantic efforts to call her friends, but none wanted to get involved in the crisis; she eventually called James, Idiok's best friend who came immediately to her rescue. James was touched when he saw Uduak arranging her scattered belongings on the street, weeping. He challenged Idiok and Rose for the disgraceful and immature way they had handled the misunderstanding. James, while helping Uduak into his car, told his friend to come over to his house to discuss when he (Idiok) had calmed down. James, a Medical Doctor, considered Uduak's injuries and took her first to his Clinic for treatment before taking her to his home, where a room had been prepared for her on his instructions.

James, a widower, had known Idiok for over 30 years –
from kindergarten years. He wondered what had gone into his
friend's head. He had supported them on their trek in search
of a child and found that there were no known medical reasons for the child-drought in his friends' marriage. About five
years ago, he had advised Idiok and Uduak to adopt a child,
but Idiok had shut it down. However, James remained optimistic that Uduak and Idiok will have a child at God's time.
Each time he celebrated the birth of any of his children, he
saw the pain and discomfort Idiok experienced but continued
to pray for his friends. Thus, taking everything in, James concluded that his friend is 'demonized' and wondered where the
love of more than 20 years had gone…

At the Clinic, he had requested for a comprehensive medical assessment to be done because Uduak looked very frail
and malnourished. He also suspected that Uduak had not been
taking good care of herself under the circumstances. When
the laboratory results came in, he realized that, in addition,
the Laboratory Technician had conducted a pregnancy test,
which came out positive. He was very excited about this and
drove home to a still depressed Uduak. Uduak brightened up
on seeing an excited James, asking if he won one of the many
contracts he had been working on. "Udy, this is bigger than
any financial award. Why didn't you tell me that you were
pregnant? I could have mistakenly given you a medication
that would affect the baby…"

Uduak did not believe him, "James, I no longer have any
hope of that; please, do not taunt me or open those wounds
that are healing. Now that your friend has thrown me out,

please start working on the adoption process your friend abandoned. Pregnancy? Please… for 20 years I prayed to God, I am in my late 40s… please, perish that thought. I am not pregnant." Patiently, James explained what happened at the Clinic and how the Laboratory Technician went beyond his brief to include a pregnancy test with a positive outcome. Uduak insisted on independent tests, and all came out with the same results. She begged James to protect the information, vacillating between telling Idiok and keeping her pregnancy a secret.

Unable to keep quiet in the light of discovery, Uduak called her mother for an urgent discussion. Uduak's mother was concerned that her daughter asked her to come to James' home. She knew 'something was wrong', yet promptly responded to the call. Uduak received her mother with the joyous news, but could not dismiss the anxiety on her mother's face. She took her mother to her room and described her ordeal in the past one year. Uduak's mother was quick to note that God had blessed her for the physical abused meted out to her by her husband weeks back. She admonished her to keep quiet on the pregnancy, whilst extracting the same commitment from James.

Uduak focused on her job with new zeal, aware that her responsibilities would increase with the coming baby. Her relationship with James remained respectful and cordial. James treated her like a co-owner of the home and the domestic staff referred to her as 'new mistress of the house'. Several efforts made by Uduak to leave the house were resisted, with James positing her 'fragile nature as a late bloomer'. Her mother

supported James' position for the sake of the baby and prayed
for her daughter's safe delivery.

Two weeks to Uduak's expected date of delivery, during
breakfast, the security man notified James and Uduak of a
visitor. Uduak managed to navigate herself carefully to open
the door and found an emaciated and tired Idiok. Before she
could recover from the shock, Idiok shoved Uduak aside,
gave her a scornful look and headed straight to engage James
in a fistfight. He accused his friend of betrayal and impreg-
nating his wife. James was quick to remind him that he sent
his wife disgracefully out of the house; Idiok was beyond reason. Uduak took a seat far from the dueling duo for safety as
her weak efforts to explain to her estranged husband that
James did not betrayed any trust, but had been a gentleman
and a good friend throughout her stay with him. All pleas fell
on deaf ears; James and Idiok's drivers and two security
guards later disengaged the brawling friends. Idiok later
stomped out of the compound cursing.

Uduak who, again, attempted to calm Idiok was pushed
aside. Uduak fell down on her side and started bleeding. In
spite of his serious bruises, James rushed a hysterical Uduak
to a nearby hospital for urgent medical attention. James, well
known by the hospital management provided all the required
medical information and support during the emergency
birthing process. Uduak was delivered of a set of the most
adorable twins I have seen; James was excited and showcased
the twins with pride as if they were his.

Uduak's mother, who arrived promptly to take care of her

daughter, insisted that Idiok needed to be appropriately informed that he is the biological father of the children. Reluctantly, James accompanied Uduak's mother to Idiok's home. Idiok coldly received them, but was elated after Uduak's mother and James explained his paternity of the children. He requested James to return Uduak and his children to their 'rightful home immediately'; Uduak's mother disagreed, stressing that her visit was appropriate to ensure that Idiok and Rose stopped the 'character assassination'. The couple floated the story Uduak who was chased out of her matrimonial home because of adultery.

Meanwhile, during the months Uduak lived in his house, James developed warm feelings towards her – something more than intimate friendship. Having been widowed for over eight years, James did not consider the need to remarry or be romantically involved with any woman. His love for Lydia was so intense that after her death, the thought of another woman never crossed his mind; James had thrust himself into his medical practice and other charity activities. To him, Uduak is *special* – beyond her physique, she is charming, virtuous and homely. James saw in Uduak the perfect home manager and life partner; he had prayed and periodically fasted for divine help to marry the mother of twins. Idiok rejected all peace entreaties for Uduak's return to her matrimonial home.

On Uduak's part, her rejection by Idiok was very disappointing when she considered the 20 years they lived as man and wife. She wondered where the considerate and loving Idiok had gone. Although Idiok was against adoption, his attitude to her was always loving and caring. He had continued to believe that they would be blessed with children – 'at God's time'. Now, she was also aware of the emotional bond that was growing between her and James.

James was a complete gentleman who could melt any woman's heart. His relationship with Idiok, his lifelong friend had been cut off for no fault of his own. He was involved in a triangle in which he was only an accidental player - his only guilt was responding to Uduak's distress call. Following Idiok's rejection, James had respectfully courted Uduak, but had the integrity to understand her silent restraints. Nothing emotional could happen between them until she divorced Idiok, who had asked for a divorce. Uduak believed that something was wrong with her husband whom she had lived with for over 20 years. However, James had become a constant variable in her life, while she seamlessly infused into his family. His children respected her and consulted with her on some academic and domestic challenges. Uduak was indeed the 'Lady in Charge'; interestingly, James' children addressed Uduak's twins "our little brothers".

Attending the Christening of Uduak's 'Golden Twins' as some Church Mothers called them was an exciting experience for me. Idiok refused to attend his children's Christening, excusing himself on health grounds. The Christening took place at the Church were Idiok and Uduak were joined in Holy Matrimony; it was also the parish where the 'once upon a time happy couple' had fellowshipped for more than 20 years. Blessing the twins was precise and testimonies followed – an emotionally broken Uduak could not express her happiness.

Everyone understood what she had gone through – pain, pity, rejection, segregation, humiliation – you conceive it, and you will note the points in her married life that Uduak was at that rung of the dejection ladder.

Midway into the program, Idiok's aunt led family members, including Idiok's mother to ask for forgiveness and prevail on Uduak to return home. Idiok's mother confessed that her actions were based on the frustration of a loving mother who desired to enjoy the warmth of her grandchildren. She further stated that Rose could not have children because of multiple abortions resulting to ruptured womb.

Stripped of shame, Uduak respectfully thanked her mother in-law, but insisted that her children would return to one who gave her shelter and saved her from Idiok's disgraceful rejection. Intervention by church leaders gave way for the Pastor to round up the thanksgiving session. The conflict for Uduak and James had begun. Throughout the rest of the service, Uduak pondered on what returning to her previous life would 'feel' like. Again, why did her mother in-law suddenly want her back? She had lived outside her matrimonial home for over 10 months – almost a year! Could the birth of her children bring back the love she and Idiok once had? Uduak pondered for the thousandth time.

James was so emotionally distraught that he went outside the church to clear his head. He had his eyes shut with head down as I reached him with a tap on his shoulder. He suddenly looked 10 year older from the man who invited me for a thanksgiving celebration. You can never imagine the deteriorating effects of emotional turmoil. Ill-expressed or un-vented emotions can have life threatening impact on an individual. James as a medical doctor should know. He had planned that after the reception at home, he would ask Uduak to marry him. To woo a virtuous woman like Uduak, James knew that he needed to allow her enough time to deal with issues regarding her husband. Now that she is being urged to return to Idiok's house, James felt he had lost her – and stepped out to clear his head.

"Why don't you tell her how you truly feel about her? James, why do you prefer to punish yourself and hurt your health? If Uduak does not have any feelings for you, she would have left your house because she can afford an apartment of her own…" I scolded my friend and physician. "You don't understand, Nellie", he said in a whisper. "If she leaves me, I will die. I love her with all my heart... I have kept my distance because I know what she went through these last one year. She had enough problems, especially dealing with a pregnancy at 50. Her health deteriorated and she needed the best care to get her groove back - Uddy battled with high blood pressure, pneumonia and asthma. When you tell a woman you love her under such circumstances, she would think you love her out of pity or plainly taking advantage of the situation at hand... Whatever tomorrow brings, I will always love her."

Reception at James' home was well organized as his children supported; they ensured that all the guests were attended to. One could not but observe that Uduak was withdrawn and very quiet amidst the music and merriment. Perceptive friends knew she was mentally preoccupied and emotionally drained. She had a permanent 'plastic smile' on, greeting and attending to her guests – colleagues, friends, in-laws, James' friends and some hospital staff. She walked past me absent-mindedly and almost fell. I helped steady her, and, holding her by the hands, we walked into the kitchen. "You need a break, Uduak," I said like a stern headmistress. I gave her a glass of warm milk and asked her to sit down. Embarrassingly, tears streamed down Uduak's cheeks and she sobbed uncontrollably. I reached out to James' daughter Veronica who advised we take Uduak to her (Veronica's) bedroom through the back entrance.

Veronica, 26, then a final year medical student said, "Auntie, she is suffering so much. She and my dad love each other but decided to punish themselves. She is like a mother to me; I know the intimate things I share with her. I trust and love her like a mother, but she believes that Uncle Idiok will come running to her because she now has children. What she has closed her eyes to is the humiliation that man put her through. You don't disrespect anyone you love – fertile or not. People marry for better or worse…" Turning to Uduak, she said, "Mom, you are not going back to that house. We love you and Daddy loves you more. Uncle Idiok's attitude towards you cannot change because of our 'golden twins'." Veronica reached down to hug Uduak and left the room.

People who know me understand that I am usually not patient with anyone displaying irrational behaviour, however justified. Uduak clearly was being childish and unrealistic, but, with matters of the heart, intelligence is usually not enough. When she was ready to speak, it was almost a soliloquy, just rhetorical questions:

'What is the worth of a virtuous life? How can love be a lie? Why should the lack of a child or children matter in marriage if there is true love? Is love a myth or reality? Why couldn't he attend his own children's christening? Oh, God, why am I confused when the issues are crystal clear? What did we have for 20 years of marriage – love or lust? Did I grow out of shape? Rose…. what was the real reason you broke my home? James, I am so sorry…"

It was only an emotional expression, but clearly a session to vent from her emotional entrapment. "Uduak, you are torturing yourself; this self-inflicted wound is truly unnecessary. God has rewarded you for years of marital servitude; yes, that was what those 20 years of your life was. I have gathered enough testimony to conclude that you lived a lie – pleasing, enduring and serving without complaint. You stayed true to your vows, but you know best if your husband was. Everyone who loves you is concerned about you. The direction of the pendulum of your life is significant – Idiok or James; you are old enough to know that children need warmth and love to grow right. Deep within you, there is not an iota of doubt as to who truly loves you UNCONDITIONALLY. Anyone who puts conditions in a marriage in which children are late in coming does not love unconditionally. The worst marriage is that in which a woman is emotionally and mentally tortured – and abused because she wants to stay married. You cannot stay with an illusion forever… This emotionally triangulated farce needs to end.

"A quick question for you, Uduak: Do you think Idiok's family would have come running to you if Rose had had a child for Idiok? A man who is truly in love with a woman will apologize for his wrong deeds; true love is not proud. I believe you already have the answer within you, but you are afraid to deal with the consequences. Our hearts never lie to us, but out mind can sometimes be weak to respond to what the heart steers towards. Pray about everything and ask God for divine wisdom and courage to carry through what is best for you and the children. Do not act out of pity, but you must fight the rear-view mirror mentality. Rear-view mirror images are depressing and ensures you stay rooted in the miry clay of sadness and emotional servitude." Giving her a copy of my call card, I called on Veronica to take care of Uduak and left the ceremony quietly.

Two months later, I had just returned from a fieldwork in the Niger Delta region when the mailroom coordinator handed me a registered mail. He assured me that it had been scanned as required. The content of the mail was pleasantly surprising. Enclose in a special envelop were a handwritten letter from Uduak and a wedding invitation as 'Special Guest' – James and Uduak were finally getting married. The content of the letter was inspiring:

Emotional Nellie,

I want to thank you for removing the heavy veil from my eyes during our brief meeting. You may not understand what you did, but talking to me the way you did opened my eyes to the FACT that for 20 years I had lived a lie. I idolized Idiok and accepted everything he dished out to me. Growing up, I was told that marriage is to be endured, no matter the circumstances. My parents were happily married till my father passed on, but my mother told me that a woman had to take all sorts in order to keep her home – simply put, to make my marriage work, I needed to accept every ill treatment meted out to me.

True Love is unconditional; I have come to the realization (albeit late) that any marriage without that element will eventually fail. I know that many people are covering the real situations in their homes for fear of a divorce. During the last 10 years of marriage without a baby to show, my husband had played the field with several women. I continued to justify his infidelity as my fault since he was desperately searching for a child; I even prayed for his girlfriends to get pregnant. Only his cousin, Akan, who lived with us knew what I went through in that hell called marriage.

*Idiok's marriage to Rose opened my eyes to the fact that our marriage vows meant nothing to him, especially amid the fights, insults and intense denials. When I was violently taken by my beloved husband that frightful night, I felt like someone who was run over by a heavy-duty truck. Idiok violated me like a team of ten gangsters mercilessly raping me simultaneously. That night was the longest night of my life as I was overcome with pains; I felt as heavy as a 30-ton truck afterwards. I did not know that God would reward my pain with these bundles of joy; their names are also symbolic **Samuel** and **Solomon.***

I thank God for the blessing of my midlife soul mate, James. I never knew what being loved meant until James came into my life. He was my knight in shining armour who saved me from the dungeon of depression and dejection. I was emotionally trapped in the prison of denial and oppression. With a show of gentleness and kindness, James made me to feel loved again. Ours is a relationship based on openness, trust and love – and blessed by God. In James, I understand why God established the sacred matrimony – and the meaning of 'two becoming one'.

I realize today that love based on an external entity is futile. A third person or persons cannot be the basis for happiness in a marriage designed for two people. A child is God's Special Gift, which comes at His own Time. If God had blessed me with children at the early stages of my marriage, I would not have discovered the truth about the man I married for over 20 years. My life is an experience I wish others to learn from; no matter how dark the night is, dawn will surely come – and with it, the rising of the sun... Thus, I give Him all the Glory."

James and Uduak's wedding ceremony was a private affair – solemn and simple, with Veronica as the Chief Bridesmaid. Nevertheless, the hall was filled with blessing, prayers and joy unspeakable. Together, the two have begun to live their lives again.

Emotional Piggy Bank

Everyone in relationship faces one form of emotional triangle or the other – a friend, foe, colleague, child, etc. The problem begins when the longevity or success of your marriage or relationship is dependent on them. External relationships ought to complement not DETERMINE your marriage.

Understanding emotional processes swirling around us is critical; it is helpful in steering us towards what I call *emotional objectivity* when dealing with intense situations. To survive life's complexities occasioned by emotional triangles, we must search within us to establish some degree of emotional dependence and interdependence. These elements help to define our sensitivities and rationality.

Self-realization helps the individual to establish emotional vulnerability and strength. It is the first step in determining the texture of your emotional balance. Uduak's emotional rationalization came twenty years of emotional abuse, steadily weakening any attempt to emotionally emancipate from death-pool of low self-esteem.

Unfortunately, available relationship guides are generic at best – drawing lessons learned subjects of research. Thus, the individual needs to deal with his or her emotional situations to determine resolution processes that work. Each person has a unique story; hence, emotional emancipation in hurtful relationships rests completely on the party affected.

6

Episode 6

Class Clash: Triumph of True Love
Transformed by Love's Influence: What is the 'Class' of Love?

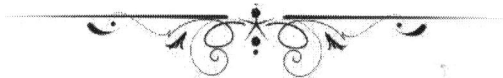

Class clashes are present in all communities, but we only hear it to the extent that each family desires publicity. My favourite class clash was the celebrated marriage of Prince Charles and Princess Diana (of blessed memory). In that near Cinderella story, individual families debated on whether the marriage will be successful or not. The determination of two people from extreme backgrounds 'joining in holy matrimony' was thrilling to the world. The couple was determined in their love, and eventually actualized their dreams. Two handsome gentlemen are the fruits of the love between Prince Charles and late Princess Diana. This reflection on cross-class unions depict that in spite of challenges and complications intertwined in such relationships, there have been accounts of many cross-class unions that have succeeded – and still strong.

The adage "birds of a feather flock together", which is based on the 'phenomenon' that people with similar interests and values are attracted, conflicts the scientific principle that "opposites attract". It has been noted that 'social class' can influence individual interests and values, impacting relationships – positively or negatively. Although social status is not the only influence on relationships, it does play a significant role, depending on the emotional maturity of the personalities involved.

Sociologically, Social Class refers mainly to 'economic status' and foundational background of an individual, or the 'economic status of your parents'. Judy Kilpatrick, a London based licensed mental health therapist, posits, "Individuals within a particular social class generally share common experiences, such as a similar level of education and type of work. Although there is great variability within a social class, people who grow up in a particular environment are likely to share the interests and values of their parents or the community in which they were raised. "Values are shaped by many influences, such as your family, culture and life experiences. People with similar values often share common political and religious views. These views determine the way you think people should be treated and the kinds of activities you enjoy.

Although people from the same social class often share values, people from different social classes can have common values, providing a relationship with a strong basis".

In her book *The Power of the Past,* sociologist Jessi Streib shows that marriages between someone with a middle-class background and someone with a working-class background can involve differing views on all sorts of important things—child-rearing, money management, career advancement, how to spend leisure time. In fact, couples often overlook class-based differences in beliefs, attitudes, and practices until they begin to cause conflict and tension...When it comes to attitudes about work, people who were raised middle-class are often very diligent about planning their career advancement. They map out long-term plans, meet with mentors, and take specific steps to try to control their career trajectories. People from working-class backgrounds were no less open to advancement, but often were less actively involved in trying to create opportunities for themselves, preferring instead to take advantage of openings when they appeared."

The limited extrapolation from Streib's research outcome presents the visible and invisible behavioural challenges inherent in cross-class matches. Actors who are involved in a cross-class challenge can significantly shift from projected doom outcome based on their individual and collective maturity and openness to many doom predictions. Beyond the primary actors, family preferences, values, practices and lifestyle from both families, play important role in ensuring a successful relationship or in whipping up negative sentimentalities that may affect positive outcome.

The emotional trial of Richard and Hadiza was one that caused me a major paradigm shift because of its complexities. It was a blend of cross-class, cross-religion and economic variations. Trapped in the prism of social expectations and family value-conflicts, the duo must make a decision on the longevity of their relationship. Richard, the only son of petty traders, managed to finish secondary school with straight 'As' in all the subjects. Regardless of his excellent results, his parents could not afford the cost of tertiary education. A young Richard later got a messenger job at his uncle's company and began saving for his university education. At 25, he got admission to study Business Administration in of the Federal Universities. University education was a struggle for him because he had to support himself to obtain basic amenities and study aids. He could not afford full accommodation, so he had to squat with friends from time to time. Richard soon became a well-known 'mobile boarder'; he supported himself by 'coaching' fellow students in some subjects and assignments for a 'small fee'.

At his faculty, Richard was noted as a very bright student; he was every lecturer's 'research assistant'; this exposure gave him access to educational materials, which he maximally utilized. For his productivity, his lecturers were happy to lend him books for private study; he spent all spare moments studying at the School Library. It was not surprising that at the end of his study, he won several departmental and faculty awards as Overall Best Faculty Student with First Class Degree. After his National Youth Service year, Richard was 'spot hired' by a Commercial Bank as a Student Graduate

Intern. It was during there that he met Hadiza who Her...
Hadiza smiled, bid him goodbye and walked away a happy
customer.

Hadiza was known as a difficult customer and every senior
bank official did his or her best to avoid her. It was on record
that three officials had been sacked, queried or redeployed for
disrespecting Hadiza and her siblings. Her father was the
Chairman of the Board of Directors of the Bank. Hadiza had
waltzed into the bank with two bodyguards and a personal assistant. The Internal Controls Manager, Mr. Briggs, buzzed
Richard to attend to 'the young lady speedily.' He wondered
why his boss had included 'speedily', but raising his head, he
understood. Standing at the center of the banking hall was a
paragon of beauty whose gesture indicated that she was
'pissed off'. His colleagues shook their heads in pity, con-
cluding that Richard will be another victim of 'Chairman's
spoilt children'.

Richard put on his most professional composure, walked to
her, extending a hand in greeting. Hadiza gave him a sweeping look and asked who he was. With confidence, he responded, "I am Richard. How may I be of help?" The
soft-spoken, respectful, confident and professional manner
got to Hadiza, who was used to people fuzzing all over her.
Bemused by impressed, she asked, "Do you know who I
am?" Richard gave her a customer-friendly breath-taking
smile, "Of course. You are my customer and I wish to know
how I can be of service to you." Without waiting for her response, he steered her to a comfortable seat. There was pin
drop silence in the banking hall. Hadiza was well known to
be dramatic and difficult. Everyone wondered when she

would erupt like a volcano; Richard listened to her complaint, checked the system, and explained key processes to Hadiza. She took some notes, made some calls, signed two cheque leaves and handed them to Richard.

Richard walked to the counter, picked up a deposit slip and returned to his desk, and handed the form to Hadiza. Like a subdued lion, she filled out he form and handed over to Richard, who stamped it and returned the customer copy to her. She stood up and extended her hand for a handshake. Richard gave her a warm but professional handshake; he was about sitting down when Hadiza opened her purse and gave Richard her call card. He was seen gesturing that he had none to give her, but wrote his details on a post-it note pad, tore it and handed over to

Mr. Briggs summoned Richard to his office; he was apprehensive as he did not hear the earthquake or get a scolding call from the Managing Director. As Richard stepped into Mr. Briggs' office, he was greeted with queries, "What happened out there?" "Was Madam Hadiza upset?" "What did you do wrong?" "Am I supposed to be happy?" Richard was taken aback in confusion, "Sir, I don't understand. Miss Hadiza was attended to as directed and has gone. Is there any problem, Sir?" It dawned on Mr. Briggs that Richard did not know the real identity of who he had attended to. "Miss Hadiza is Chairman's daughter. She is known to be problematic; mismanaging her has caused some people their jobs in the past. There is no known strategy to handle her. So, all my unit heads were afraid when we go notice that she was coming to reconcile her accounts. I am sorry Richard, I should have informed you…"

Richard was surprised and mentally reviewed how he had handled the 'customer'. He assured Mr. Briggs that everything would be all right because Miss Hadiza left as a satisfied customer. Walking back to his seat, he wondered why he had been pushed forward as the 'fall guy'; he then silently said a prayer of thanks to God for wisdom in managing this 'troublesome customer'. Richard continued to deal with daily deliverables with extra caution after that day, making sure that he did not inadvertently enter any stormy waters. Just as he won the admiration of his supervisors in managing difficult clients, he also became the object of envy by his co-interns who did not see 'anything special' about him. Richard noted their change of behaviour towards him, but he focused on his tasks at work and at home. He needed this internship to keep food on the table and cater for his two siblings; his mother's health has been failing more frequently.

Five weeks later, on a very wet Friday afternoon, coming out the conference room to his workstation, Richard was surprised to see Hadiza seating by his desk; on recalling all the warnings he got from his bosses about her, his countenance changed. Putting on a bland expression, he greeted her and asked if she had been attended to. Hadiza noticed a change in attitude; she was enraged, but managed to speak slowly, "They have told you about me, right? Richard, you are an intelligent young man and should be able to decipher truth from lies. Yes, I am quick tempered, but I would only be upset if someone gives me a good reason to do that. You did not treat me like 'Chairman's daughter'. You dealt with me as a 'customer'; I respect people who are professional, not those who

kiss my feet because I am my father's child. That is syco-
phancy; I hate it... The last time I came to this branch, you
made me to fill out my deposit form and followed due
process. Your colleagues will fill out my form, make stupid
mistakes and tremble for nothing...that is eye service. I
loathe such behaviour." She paused for effect. "Do we understand each other now? I hate to be reminded that I am the
Chairman's daughter. I am a customer, an account owner and
should be regarded as that. There is no title here for sons and
daughters of Chairman or Managing Director..."

Richard, humbled by Hadiza's perspective, wondered why
Hadiza would be offended by preferential treatment; why
would Hadiza not want preferential treatment in a bank in
which her father has majority shares? Would he be that humble if he was in Hadiza's shoes? Not really, he was honest
about the fact that it was tempting to be prideful under the circumstances. Observing his confusion, Hadiza resumed her
venting, "Have you ever lived with a label all your life? Some
people think it is a wonderful thing, but I think otherwise. It
is difficult to get true and worthy friends who do not see your
background first; I want to be seen as Hadiza without ap-
pendages. That is the reason you won my heart last time. You
were courteous and professional; you resolved my issues
without reference to my family name – in fact, the surname
meant nothing to you. You dealt with me as a CUSTOMER.
Please do not allow people who lack personal confidence turn
you into a robotic staff. God forbid it. Please Richard, for you
own sake, don't let them fill your head with nonsense. Who-
ever comes into this bank is in need of service, please serve
the person the way you resolved my issues last time – profes-

sionally. That is secret to customer retention – not eye service… By the way, should my father come in here, please respectfully attend to him; my father does not like people
falling over him in 'fake respect'."

Richard took everything in like a student in a lecture theatre. Hadiza spoke as an idealist; but the world is not for idealist. Within a short period, he had come to learn that 90% of
the classroom learning is far from the reality in the 'real
world'. You cannot survive the Banking and Finance world
on 'Professionalism' alone; you need home and street wisdom
– in addition to Professor Robert Greene's *48 Laws of Power.*
He tried to infuse Hadiza's lecture into the appropriate com-
partment of his strategies for survival. He was lost in his personal reverie when Hadiza called him back to reality. He was
angling for more lessons but was surprised by Hadiza's request: "I am aware that you have been struggling to get you
ACCA because a First Class degree is not enough to survive
this industry. Many of your superiors do not have a first degree but the ACCA and years of experience give them advantage. Yes, that is the reality of this industry – your degree
without the required certifications will lead to a frustrating
career. I am also struggling with it; I am requesting that you
become my study companion…" Richard was terrified, stam-
mering in response, "Ehm… Madam, sorry, Mrs. …No, Miss
Hadiza, I am sorry I will not be able to do that. You see I have
a sick mother, and two siblings that I support after work. I am
just an intern. I don't even have the money to register… it is
in Pounds Sterling. I cannot afford it for now…Please, I am
sorry to disappoint you…"

Hadiza gave him a reassuring smile that calmed him. Calmly she said, "I am aware of all that you have said. You need to understand that I am desperate. I need to get my certifications before I become an employee in this bank. I have my MBA from Internationally recognized Ivy League School, but I need to deal with the local realities. I am not going to depend on my father's position to get employment. I need to be competitive. Therefore, my offer is this: Teach me for a special fee; I will pay for your registration and take care of your mother's health and provide minimal support to your siblings. To reassure you of my intentions, the study center will be very close to your house. You will give me two hours coaching every Saturday and Sunday at your convenience."

Richard was tempted to agree with the arrangement immediately, because it was a Heaven-sent opportunity that comes once in a lifetime. How could he refuse such an opportunity for an international certification? He had been studying for the different modules and could comfortably excel in the examinations, but his handicap had been finance. All his meager earnings as an Intern went to his mother and siblings. He had taken the role of the family since his father died during his second year in the university. Richard knew the request was a piece of cake for him (not by his might, but God had been good to him). However, he needed to clear his head; for, this could be a dream or temptation. As a priority task, he had to speak with his mother who, as his 'spiritual adviser', would pray over this opportunity. He made efforts to conceal his excitement as he replied Hadiza, "Can you give me a couple of days to think about this? You know this means a 100% change in my schedules, plans and programs... Let me revert…" Hadiza interrupted, "Sure. I will call you on Monday at your lunchtime. Is that okay?" As Richard sheepishly nodded, Hadiza heading towards the EXIT door, waltzed out of the building.

Richard's mother was unusually deeply thoughtful on receiving the 'full package' of Hadiza's proposal. She had religious and class concerns: What is a non-Christian proposing to her son? Again, what does a rich girl want with her son, when she can easily afford the best professors in the world? Conversely, this may be answer to her prayers for 'Divine Favour' for her son. After all, God created everyone equal; class differentiation is not of God. This was a 'blessing' that God had brought straight to her son; Richard had not asked for the opportunity, Hadiza had a need and God brought her to her son who had 'what she wanted'. Richard's mother ruminated this matter all weekend.

After dinner on Sunday night, she called her son to her room; her words were brief but deep: "My son, you are a grown man and understand your personal needs and family expectations. Many times, your aspirations have been sacrificed at the altar of family needs. This time God is about rewarding you for your sacrifices and selflessness. You must ensure that you do not disappoint the young lady who is submitting to the will of God for us. However, I need to meet with her for a brief chat to clarity some concerns I have about this arrangement."

Richard was elated that his mother had given the issue a very serious thought, but his major concern is that his home (a two-room apartment) may not meet their study needs.

From office 'news mills' he heard the Chairman lived in a mansion within the high profile residential areas; he wondered how Hadiza would view where he lived. He was comforted that it was Hadiza that gave the conditions, thus she should have done some 'research' before coming out with such a plan. He would stick to the terms and conditions because he was not ashamed of his humble background. He looked forward to the next day; twelve hours now seemed like eternity.

Richard attacked his early morning tasks with a new vigour, aware that his colleagues looked at him in a 'funny' way. Hadiza did not give him a specific time for her affirmation visit; when lunchtime was over, he was disappointed that he had been stood up. He silently thanked God because he had kept the information to himself, and everyone believed that Hadiza's last visit was official. He brushed aside the study arrangement as a mirage and completed his day's task. He was therefore taken aback when Hadiza called him at exactly 1715hours and asked him to meet her at an eatery two blocks away. Richard reminded her that he needed to be on the first staff bus, which was scheduled to depart in 15 minutes. Hadiza assured him that the discussion would be brief; he was concerned that the 'study deal' might be called off. He quickly locked up his workstation drawers and rushed to meet Hadiza. Richard quickly relayed his mother's desire to meet with her over the planned study and was surprised when Hadiza said she planned on visiting his residence to evaluate suitability.

Richard felt uneasy as they drove onto the uneven roads

that led to his residence. For the first time he noted the pools of water and potholes, old roofing sheets and electric wire that dangled dangerously on their path. Again, with embarrassment, he observed that cloth lines were close to the street and had weathered under-wears laid out shamelessly on the old fences. As they inched closer to his compound, he advised that Hadiza parks about 20 meters from his residential compound. Hadiza was calm, trying to gently navigate through the muddy road and dodging one pothole after the other. She reassured Richard that her SUV could wade through any terrain, eventually parking in front of Richards' compound. A frail and lean middle-aged woman was sitting in front of the compound, enjoying the evening air. Hadiza saw the striking resemblance and parked carefully near her. "Good evening Ma," she greeted alighting from her car, while Richard followed in tow like a drenched duck.

Hadiza's respectful and cheery manner brought Richard's mother back from her reverie. "I am Hadiza, Richard's friend", she introduced herself. Sheepishly, Richard apologized for not notifying his mother as he was taken unawares. Richard's mother warmly steered the duo though the dark passage into the sitting room. "We didn't prepare for you, but we have a bottle of water though not cold", she said offering Hadiza a bottle of SWAN Bottled Water. "'Thank you, Ma," Hadiza took the bottle, uncapped it and drank thirstily. Richard was shocked because the bottle was warm as there had not been power all day. Richard's mother was a very practical woman, who needed to have the discussion over with. She asked Hadiza directly: "Why do you want to study with my son when you can afford any lecturer or professor?"

Hadiza was impressed with her diction and could tell that she had some education. When she spoke, Richard's mother was in awe… "Your son is smart and reminds me of my father before he became somebody. He has so much hidden potential waiting to be harnessed. I am not Mother Theresa; I want someone I can challenge to success as much as I personally desire excellence. When I met Richard, he did something nobody had ever done; he brought me down to the level of a 'peasant'. That was thought provoking, because I was rudely reminded that we are all equal. I did some finding on his personal life, and someone at the bank told me he had been saving for the ACCA Certification. This coincided with what I am currently struggling with. So, I decided to partner with him for two reasons: first, to encourage him to continue being professional, and, two, to open another channel for him to make money and get certified too. I am aware that he holds lessons for some people; I want to co-study with the group. His payment will be by way of funding the program; I believe that we shall come out successful."

"Why have you chosen my home as the lesson venue?" Richard asked petulantly. "To give you control, and to reassure your mother that my intentions are good. I am also aware that you hold the lessons at weekend in this sitting room," Hadiza replied. Hadiza intrigued Richard's mother; she had expected some loopholes in her answers; she had envisaged that Hadiza would look at them condescendingly. She realized that she had been trapped in the same bait that she planned to ensnare Hadiza and free her son from her 'clutches'. Instead, she found a down-to-earth, unassuming and humble girl determined to make a difference in the life of her son in a dignified manner. She knew that Hadiza had the means to give Richard any sum for the program, but she had chosen a path that would give her son dignity. She knew that Hadiza was also discerning and clever, but worried for her safety to and fro the impoverished neighbourhood dominated by hoodlums. Reluctantly, she acceded, on the condition that lesson sessions are scheduled early during the weekends to enable Hadiza travel in daylight. In spite of her doubts, she admitted that Hadiza was a well-bred girl who would have a positive influence on her son and give him the right career boost.

During the months that followed, Hadiza's weekends were dedicated to her professional certification project. They studied in a group of five drawing from each other's strengths and strengthening areas of knowledge gap. The team agreed to do a full-throw by taking all the papers within a 'diet' season. The last few weeks was intensive forcing Richard to apply for a vacation, which was approved by Mr. Briggs. When the results came, all team members were successful. This was a miraculous feat because the team members later nicknamed **"Fast Five"**, as first timers. Hadiza had become known in the neighbourhood that even the hoodlums respected her because she was not snotty or prideful. She mixed freely and was attentive to their needs without compulsion. She gained more popularity the day she helped a woman in labour to the hospital while her husband was away; she bought gifts for mother and child after safe delivery.

Gradually, Richard and Hadiza became inseparable; however, she respected his work and ceased visiting Richard's Branch and sent her assistants to interface with the Branch, while Richard continued to provide professional guidance. Many officers were relieved that the 'fiery Hadiza no longer visited the Branch; Mr. Briggs officially made Richard the contact point for all issues and requests from "The Chairman's Family". As Richard flawlessly handled all assignments directed to him, his visibility continued to rise. One fateful Wednesday afternoon, Richard rushed out to pick some snacks because he was so busy that he lost track of time for company. Stepping out of the office, a truck failed breaks and careened towards him and two other customers – flinging them to the hard road. Richard blacked out for many days in coma; the hospital continued to run tests to ascertain the extent of damage. Hadiza visited him every day, praying for him to regain consciousness.

On the eighteenth day, at about 0300 hours, Richard stirred and weakly opened his eyes; Hadiza was sleeping on the chair beside the bed. He was confused and tried to recall how he got to the hospital. Around him were monitors and wires attached to his head and arms. He tried to move, but the pains kept him back. He shut his eyelid hard, willing himself to remember. Nothing… Blank. Again, he opened his eyes and scanned the room, 'this is not a general ward,' he thought. 'How much will be hospital bill cost? My mother…where is she? What is Hadiza doing here? How did I get here…?' He attempted raising his head but it was strapped with something he could not see; his head hurt very much. The whole place was quiet and he could hear the ticking of the wall clock; it was 4 O'clock in the morning. He managed to clear his throat to shout for help, but only a weak sound came out, yet it was audible enough to stir Hadiza who jumped up. "Oh, thank

God…thank God you are awake. Oh, my God, thank you."
She ran out of the room in tears and returned shortly with the
Medical Director, Dr. Craig. "He just woke up, Doctor…" she
said repeatedly, in tears.

Dr. Craig checked his vital signs, pressed a button by
Richard's bed and two staff nurses came in promptly. Hadiza
was directed to leave the room for the medical staff to look
Richard over. Dr. Craig was impressed that Richard could introduce himself; he recalled his work place, his family,
friends and date of birth. However, he could not recall how
the accident happened. He only remembered stepping out of
the Bank's premises and the next was waking up in a hospital
room with 'all these gadgets'. Richard believed the accident
took place the previous day, as he constantly referred 'yesterday' in his narration. Dr. Craig told him the accident was almost three weeks ago, and he had been 'in deep sleep' as a
result of the accident. He had minor bruises, but his skull was
cracked; he had undergone two surgeries and only three days
ago, another scan was done to ensure there was no damage to
his brain. "It is a miracle that you can recall most of the
events before the accident. We were concerned about your hip
disc and memory because of the physical impact of the accident. I will arrange for some specialists later this morning to
do a thorough check; we shall progress treatment from there.
Our staff will continue to monitor you."

Hadiza stayed close to the door and heard most of the con-
versations. Again, she thanked God for His Mercies;
Richard's mother had prayed all day at the hospital, while
Hadiza kept vigil at night. She always had a change over

clothing, using the convenience in the special room she had arranged in the high profile specialist hospital. Richard had been taken to a general hospital after the accident, where he had been stabilized. Hadiza had confidentially consulted with Dr. Mohammed, her family doctor, who confided that Richard's file was not encouraging and would stay in coma for an indefinite time. Dr. Mohammed made all the necessary arrangements for the transfer to Dr. Craig's Specialist Clinic because Craig had handled cases similar to Richard's. Hadiza witnessed firsthand the attention to detail and professionalism of the Clinic personnel and was convinced that Richard was in the best place. She was positive that with love, care and ceaseless prayers Richard would 'return to us'; his mother also had faith.

After the third day, Dr. Craig had told Hadiza that Hadiza did not know how to pray Richard's mother's style, but she had trust that God is universal and loved His children; He is the Merciful One. She encouraged the Clinic staff to pray for Richard "in the best ways you know possible" because "Richard must live." Many times she had wondered what was holding her bound to Richard but could not put a finger on it; she knew it was something beyond her. At some point during the last 18 days, she was finally convinced that her emotions are geared towards something stronger than her personal re-solve. Her parents knew something was 'wrong' with their daughter who had been very depressed and subdued in recent times; the light has gone out and darkness seemed to have pervaded. She was constantly late to work and would be the first to leave – yet she was not getting home. Hadiza had sacked here personal driver when it was obvious that her parents pressured the young man for information.

When overwhelmed with the thought of Richard dying, she held his immobile cold hands, robbing it vigorously, she would sob uncontrollably, expressing deep emotional thoughts within: "Richard, I love you... Oh, my God, I should have told him how much I love him... Richard, you cannot die. Not you my love... You must live for us... for our unborn children... You cannot die without knowing how much I love you...." She prayed with all the names of the Supreme Being she could remember, confident that her beloved would come 'back to consciousness again'. Richard was the type of man you could not lose; 'he is perfect one for me', she cried in desperation.

Hadiza recalled all the opportunities she had to tell him how she felt about him; she was aware that they had religious and class barriers between them. However, she trusted 'Fate' to fix their differences. The ACCA Certification study sessions were bonding time she looked forward to at that time – getting very attached to each other and enjoying a deep friendship. Each time she raised the subject of 'something growing between us, Richard would carefully navigate far from 'emotional waters'. She knew Richard struggled with the same barriers. The last time they were irresistibly close, Richard had told Hadiza: "Girl, we have the Mediterranean Sea and the Bermuda Triangle separating us; Let us not start what we cannot finish. Our parents are too set in their ways to compromise their stand – our religions in particular." This well thought-out submission convinced Hadiza that the feeling is mutual. Hadiza was sure that Richard's mother knew

about these 'feelings', which made her to 'approve' Hadiza's
unrestricted access and emotionally care for her son. More-
over, Dr. Craig advised that Richard needed to hear the voices
of people he cared about as familiar voices aid mental stability and recovery.

Now, as she walked into the Richard's hospital room,
warmness coursed through her; her smile was full of hope.
She was no longer mournful, but was light on her feet knowing that silence would no longer respond to her greetings.
Richard was propped up on the bed and looked up in anticipation, smiled and spoke weakly: "I was told that I crossed
many mountains, but too lazy to get to the top of Kilimanjaro
and Everest... I'd been gone for 18 days but it seems like just
yesterday when I was hit by a truck.... 18 days in coma?
Thank you, Merciful God... How are my mother, brother and
sister? Hadiza, what are you doing here so early? I am sorry,
but I feel twisted and sandwiched. What is happening to me?"
Hadiza was all smiles seeing Richard almost back to his hu-
morous self – always adding satire to testy situations. "My
love, I have been living here with you these past 18 days. So,
I have been co-habiting with my fallen knight in shining armour whom God brought back to me. Your family is okay;
Mama does the day watch, while I do the night watch. On
these 18 days you have been "confined to the beyond", nothing happened - you just slept the days through. It was frightful, but thank God that you are alive and conscious again. Dr.
Craig says you will need another look-over by Specialists this
morning; so I will be here to meet with them. Mama should
be here later in the day... I already informed her that you are
back to us..."

Richard had never seen Hadiza so bright and radiant before; he noted Hadiza spoke in familial language about 'Mama' and wondered 'what' she could have done to his mother to allow her spend nights in a 'confined' space with him. Flashing back to the time they were preparing for their professional certification, his mother had insisted that *Fast Five* studied in the open. This largely minimized the degree of physical contact; however, they have been in constant telephone communication. Richard knows his mother is a tough woman, who having been widowed after five years of marriage had devoted her all to bringing up her two sons and a daughter. The thought of what might have happened during the 18 days he was in coma caused goose to course through his skin. Who had changed him? Did he defecate? How was he cleaned and bathed? Who changed his boxers? Hadiza knew what he was thinking and assured him that the nursing staff took care of his 'personal hygiene'; Richard relaxed at the knowledge that Hadiza had respected his privacy, and as questions about the office and her work. He worried what Hadiza told her parents was the reason for staying out 18 nights, determined to ask her at a more auspicious time.

Hadiza was with him when Dr. Craig came into the room at 0900hours with three Specialists and three bags full of equipment. She squeezed his hand in assurance and left the room to the waiting room at the far end of the floor, knowing that his mother would arrive soon. Sitting with head bowed in faith, fear and apprehension, she prayed that there would be no negative report from these critical examinations. She was deep in thought and did not know when Richard's mother came sit beside her. Richard's mother gave her a warm hug; the two women wept in joy and anxiety. Richard's mother broke the embrace, reminding her that her God will complete the work He has started. She poured a glass of warm beverage and a sandwich; Richard mother watched Hadiza eat in silence – knowing that her thoughts are far from the breakfast. She can say without a shadow of doubt that Hadiza is a 'good girl with a good soul'; she does not belong to their class. She had warned her son many times about emotionally entangling with Hadiza or her likes as they belong to the 'high class'; differences in religion made the situation is made more challenging. Although she had grown very fond of Hadiza, she was sure that her parents would vigorously oppose a relationship with her son.

Dr. Craig interrupted the women who were consumed in their individual thoughts; he reassured them that Richard was in good health condition. "I am pleased to inform you that Richard is in miraculously good condition. It is indeed a miracle; we had thought that his spine would be seriously impacted because of the checks and tests done last week, but it is only a minor crack which is not life threatening. His head injury did not affect his brain or his nervous system. However, we need to observe him for another 48 hours; he has a serious pain on hip because of the fall. We want to observe how he walks, as well as continue with the physiotherapy to ensure holistic recovery. Madam, we need to note that Hadiza's presence did him a lot of good emotionally; Richard was able to recall some over 90% of Hadiza's 'sweet nothings' – this shows cognitively, he is fine… The nurses are assisting him change from hospital clothing to something more comfortable and appealing… However, before you see him, I need you to come with me to look over some documents for signature…"

As they walked into the pristine office, there was no doubt that Dr. Craig is a very organized man. His books were orderly arranged in the shelves according to heights and volume. His worktable was made of marble but free of clutter and neatly organized – pens, pencils, rulers, erasers, etc. Richard's mother could not help but comment, "You are indeed a very organized man, Dr. Craig; I am yet to see a Doctor's office so immaculately organized – nothing is out of place." Dr. Craig, taken aback by the candour of Richard's mother, smiled, gesturing them to sit down. He pulled out a file from the drawer and handed it over to Hadiza. He turned to Richard's mother: "I hope you do understand, Madam. We have worked with Ms. Hadiza's directive; she needs to sign off on these documents. I am aware that you appreciate all the efforts towards Richard's recovery. I called you in because something out of the ordinary took place before we could conduct the series of operations on your son. Recall that Richard it took you over 48 hours to locate where Richard was relocated. Upon arrival, he needed a stabilization surgery because one of the arteries that supply life to the brain was blocked; Richard would have died if this were not done within three to four hours. We all tried to reach you on your cellphone, but it was switched off. Hadiza made several consultations, but we were losing time. So, we got a Priest to marry them to enable her sign as spouse for the surgery. Richard is free to contest and annul the marriage – here is the certificate…" Dr. Craig pulled out another lever and handed a tick envelop to the stunned woman.

Richard's mother was shocked beyond words as she
opened the envelop with photos of the Priest appending
Richard's thumb. She saw a court affidavit by Hadiza that the
marriage was for the sole purpose of saving the life of her fi-
ancé. She felt a surge of multiple emotions – anger, fear, admiration, and anxiety. Lamely, she turned to Hadiza "Do you
understand what this means? Did you think of the implications before doing this? Why did you not mention that something this dastardly took place? Young lady, you don't
understand what you have done…" She felt a surge within her
that made her very dizzy. Dr. Craig walked over, calmed her
and gave her a bottle of malt drink. "When did you check
your glucose level, Madam? I think you need to go for medical check…" Richard's mother assured him her health is
fine, but the shock of Hadiza marrying someone who may not
have survived made her tremble. Hadiza could not understand
her 'mother in-law's' reaction, but quietly signed the papers
and handed over to Dr. Craig, promising to "effect final transfer before close of business today" and left the doctor's office
– Richard's mother still soliloquizing.

Richard was looking different now that he had changed to
something familiar; he was somehow radiant, far from the
gloomy-looking and apprehensive young man that welcomed
the Specialists. Hadiza held back the urge to run into his
arms, but held him gently and planted a kiss on his forehead.
"I see that the visit of the physicians was good for you. You
are almost ready to go home, Richie." They trapped each
other in a gaze that lasted, but Richard was the first to break

112

it, asking her to sit down, rather than towering over a 'sick man'. Hadiza obeyed, and they chatted over the positive result of the last check. Richard noted that he was unaware of the earlier prognosis hence he was happy that he did not have any life-changing injury to deal with. After a brief moment, his mother came in looking very depressed. Hadiza rose to leave, but whispered to Richard's mother to keep the information of their marriage a secret. The older woman nodded in acknowledgment and smiled at her son, who was excited to see his mother after what seemed like a night. He had worried about how his mother took the near-fatal accident; seeing her that morning, his apprehensions dissolved into thin air. Richard noted that there was something about his mother that morning; she had a confusing countenance that swung like a pendulum between sadness and excitement. "Mum, are you alright?" Richard needed to know that everything was okay at home; though his mother answered in the affirmative, Richard was concerned that his mother was worried about something, but not willing to discuss it with him. He knew his mother's countenance had something to do with Hadiza, "Mum, are you still worried about my closeness to Hadiza? Please relax, she is a good person…" His mother quickly changed the subject to talk about his siblings and neighbourhood update. About 12 noon, the nursing staff requested his mother to leave to enable him rest as directed by Dr. Craig.

Early evening, the Head Nurse came to take Richard out for the first time since he was admitted 18 days ago; he was lead to the Clinic Pent floor balcony overseeing the beach. While he sat there enjoying the receding sun that it dawned on him that this was a very expensive clinic. Looking down the car park from his vantage position, he noted that only an assortment of luxurious vehicles lined the parking lot. He wondered how his mother was able to get him to this high-brow clinic. Common sense told him that his mother could not have thought of this place. It had to be only one person. Hadiza! He experienced a panic attack: "How am I going to offset the bills? Why did my mother allow me to stay here knowing we cannot afford a place like this?" He made a mental note to speak with Dr. Craig, the Medical Director; he would beg him to arrange payment by installment. He was deep in introspection when someone tapped him on the shoulders; he turned to see Hadiza. She was looking surreal and cold as she walked to join him, leaning on the balcony railing; Hadiza was not sure what to expect, and would rather Richard led the discussion. She only hoped that his mother respected her request and kept the 'emergency marriage' secret – until the right time. However, she walked into his arms, urging him to hold her 'real tight' to be sure it was not a dream.

Hadiza, though concerned about many issues `(ranging from her parent to work), noted that Richard, but for the limp, was looking almost his old self. She noted the dark circles around his eyes, reminding her of the long days and nights they waited for him to come round. Hadiza also wondered what he would do when told about the ''emergency marriage'. Thus far, she had succeeded in 'deceiving' her parents that she had an online course with one-month virtual classes; although wary about the program, she was able to 'fool' her parents into believing that the time difference is the result of her constant absence from home. She had succeeded in breaking her personal investment with a reputable finance and Investment firm to pay Dr. Craig, who had handled the case with the highest level of tact and confidentiality. Dr. Craig had wondered why Hadiza had to marry a 'dying man' in order to save him; he told Hadiza that it would take love and Miracle to get Richard 'on the reverse gear'. Hadiza could not tell where her 'faith' came from when she urged the doctor to give it a try. Today, she felt fulfilled, not counting the financial and emotional cost. To her, the foundational basis for her actions was the deep friendship they had; Richard was more than a friend to her – she loved him indeed. She stayed in his arms for a moment longer and broke the contact to sit down, weak-kneed and looking up to him in dismay.

Richard looked at the woman he feared to love; there were too many barriers between them. He had always been afraid to upset his mother who gave everything she had to ensure he and his siblings got basic education. He could not do anything that would upset her – he knew that any serious relationship with Hadiza would upset his mother whose health was already fragile. To him, the best thing to do was love her from afar, praying that a very good man marries her. Hadiza was a wife material by every standard – but not a wife for him. He was aware that her parents had tried to marry her off to some rich men within her social circle and religion; Hadiza had insisted that she would never marry a man she did not love. According to Hadiza, her mother was a constant reminder of the results of marrying without love; she witnessed firsthand how her father disrespected her mother and has married two other wives. She loves her religion, but was not prepared to be a pun in the marriage chess game. She wanted a man for her self – to love and hold till death do them part. Though the marriage was based on 'emergency', she felt good about it; she knew it could be annulled whenever Richard got to know, but she did not care. It felt good being Mrs. Hadiza Richard – no matter how brief.

"Hey dear, you seem very far away; what is the matter? Office problems? Please not today… we are celebrating my return from 'yonder'", Richard joked; limping, he sat beside her. She asked how he was faring and steered the discussions around the accident and his 'miraculous return'. She brought out her sophisticated cellphone and showed him pictures of the accident and his stage-by-stage recovery. Richard was in awe that the man who looked mangled on the hospital bed was himself; the transformation was indeed, incredible. The connections he saw in the pictures were nothing compared with the few he was connected to when he came to. Hadiza told him how they moved from one specialist clinic to the other before coming to Dr. Craig's hospital; only Craig was courageous enough to accept Richard 'on experimental basis only'. Asked how his treatment so far had been financed, Hadiza said effort was made by a Non-Governmental Organization to contact Dr. Craig who was more concerned about saving lives; however, arrangements had been made for payment by installment. Richard thanked her for the efforts towards his recovery, promising upon full recovery to pay Dr. Craig all that was due to the Clinic. Hadiza was not happy lying to Richard; he hated lies, but that was the first logical thing that she could say to rest the issue. They were sharing thought of politics when a staff brought his mother to the Pent floor balcony; the sun had fully set and the skylines displayed the splendour of the evening. His mother was excited when she was informed that her son 'walked' (albeit with a limp) to the Pent floor balcony as she hastened to meet him. Seeing the glow on her son's face as they discussed, she decided not to disturb them and returned to the waiting room.

Richard's mother reflected on the 'picture' the saw earlier; they indeed looked like a newly wed couple on a honeymoon. Her son was relaxed and laughed heartily at Hadiza's jokes; they unconsciously held hands as chatted – it seemed so natural without pretenses. She was not in doubt that these young people are in love; their love would be a hard road to trek based on the realities before them. She knew nothing about Hadiza's parents however she was impressed about her comportment and passion. She was not talkative or a pretender; she was as practical as she was caring. To her, Hadiza's impulsive action to marry her son who was then in coma was charitable and foolish. How would you marry someone you are not sure would regain consciousness in a year's time? When she was able to locate her son after two days of search, Dr. Craig gave her no hope; he was very blunt: "Madam, this is a very bad case. We need a miracle for your son to regain consciousness on time; right now, we are still assessing the degree of his internal injuries – he is not looking good, at all. As long as he is still breathing, we cannot lose hope..." She wondered how Hadiza would 'emotionally invest' in her son under these circumstances. She concluded that Hadiza was a selfless young woman with a heart a gold; she could no longer contest that Hadiza loved her son unconditionally.

Again, she thought of the file Dr. Craig had given Hadiza

with documents to sign; she knew it had something to do with the hospital bill. Strangely, no staff member had talked with about cost of anything – she had lost count of the times she came visiting and her son is wheeled off for one test or the other. She knew that the bill would be 'murderous'! She asked aloud, addressing the empty room in desperation: How would she offset the bill? Where would she get such a loan? Where would a poor widow get help? Hadiza had done so much for her son already, so she would not ask her for further help. Determined to know how much loan she would need to offset Richard's bill, she walked over to the information desk requesting an update on her son's outstanding bill. The Account Manager checked the system and informed her that her son had no outstanding bills as his wife cleared the bills. The busy Manager continued his work, unaware of the stupefied woman standing by his office. She experienced an assault of emotions – admiration, anger, relief, and derision – all put together. "Is she trying to buy my son? Is Richard going to be Hadiza's slave? How could she pay my son's bill without talking to me about it? She was very angry because she felt Hadiza was 'throwing her weight about'. To Richard's mother, it was 'disrespectful' of Hadiza not to discuss her son's bills settling them.

In anger she raced to the balcony where she had left them; they were seated in silence. At her approach, Richard stood to greet his mother with excitement. "Mom, have you heard the good news? An NGO in which Hadiza is a member agreed to foot the bill to enable Dr. Craig and his team treat me. Isn't that great? Dr. Craig is very magnanimous to have agreed to that deal – or he is plain crazy... my hospital bill must be a couple of Millions. Don't worry, Mom, I have reassured Hadiza that we will pay back – even if it takes a lifetime!" Turning to face Hadiza, "You are the best gift that any man can pray for. I almost love you…" he teased Hadiza. She was used to his affectionate jokes; she smiled back thanking God that she could buy more time. The older woman did not buy the NGO story; she believed that Hadiza made up to story not to dent her son's ego. "But son, you don't event know how much…" she countered, but Richard was in high spirits, "Mom, it does not matter the amount, as long as I am alive and healthy, I will pay. The most important thing is for me to leave this hospital. I have my final review in two days, and everything will be history… please Mom, this is not the time to be sad…" Richard knew he had to reassure his mother, whose health had been poor, steering Hadiza and his mother towards the path to his 'room'.

Hadiza quietly regarded the man who spoke with a re-newed energy and gusto – yes, this was the man he fell in love with; the love that may never last in view of the obsta-cles before them. She still had faith in Fate fixing the matter. However, Richard's mother had recently been very cold to-wards her and this worried her. Hadiza was afraid that some-one may have told her something that made her suddenly 'reserved and cold', but Richard's fast recovery lifted her spirit and mien as they walked into the room. Shortly after mother and son settled down, she requested permission to leave on grounds that she had early meetings the next day and needed to review her presentation package. When Richard's mother offered to walk with her to the parking lot, she knew that the older woman had been looking for this opportunity to speak privately with her; she was not wrong.

Stepping out the elevator, Richard's mother found a quiet corner in the parking lot, without preamble she probed Hadiza: "My daughter, I need to know what is going on in that head of your. You told my son that an NGO was in charge of his bills, but I was told, "His wife already cleared his bills". How much did his bill come to? Standing here is a very confused mother; please tell me what is going on". Hadiza appreciated Richard's mother as she spoke out of concern; her response was calm and reassuring, "Ma'am, I have no hidden agenda other than the recuperation of my dear friend. I did what I had to do to save his life – to the best human extent possible. If I didn't prove to be his wife and waited until you were contacted, Richard would have died – he actually had a very slim chance of survival. I am happy it turned out well. The 'emergency marriage' is just a process tool and may not be valid upon his release as the annulment process is easy. If I should marry your son, I would be with the consent and blessings of my parents. They may not like the thought of their only daughter marrying out of 'our faith', but no religion or social class tells your heart whom to love. In this case, it is Richard, rest assured there is nothing to fear; I did not marry him for any other purpose other than to save his life."

Humbled by Hadiza's resilience and matured manner in addressing her concerns stunned her. One the payment of the hospital bill, Hadiza smiled, shook her head gently and responded calmly, "I have my savings and some monies with investment houses. All I had to do was break a couple of investments to make the payment... I didn't want Richard to be embarrassed because I know he didn't have the money and that could impact any progress he had made. Also, I needed to maintain his dignity with the mention of the NGO. Dr. Craig is a long time family friend who understands what I have done – though he thinks that I am crazy. When he is discharged, we can resolve the issues around all the deceptions and cost implication. But, I need you to understand that I have done everything out of my love for him." Richard's mother stood there stupefied as Hadiza bade her good night and drove off. She looked past the taillights of Hadiza's car, wondering what would happen if Richard was told that he was a married man. How would Hadiza's parents react when they find out that their daughter had married a dying man to save him? What was going on in Hadiza's head to have done that? She walked solemnly back to check on her son.

Five days later, Richard was discharged with a clean bill of health, but instructed to visit the hospital fortnightly for review in line with best practice. He was advised to continually stay in a cool environment because of his head injury and stay in a well-ventilated environment. His mother got a taxi to take him home, but Richard's mind was filled with how to manage the lifestyle changes that have been directed by his doctors. Traffic was light making the journey home faster than normal. As the taxi nosed into his street, a strange feeling of inadequacy whelmed over him, but looking further, he recognized Hadiza's SUV parked in front of his compound; she was discussing with his siblings and other members of the "Fast Five". Richard was excited to see his friends had organized a "Welcome Back to Life" mini-banner at the entrance to his residential compound; friends and neighbours that came to welcome him were seen helping themselves with the light refreshments on an new plastic table. Stepping into the small room that served as their sitting room, his siblings stood beside a heap of gifts and an array of get well wishes. Richard hugged his sibling with tears running down his cheeks. The show of love was overwhelming; reflecting on his near-death experience, he was convinced that life without the warmth of people you love is useless.

Hadiza was glad that Richard was loved; the open display of affection lit up the dimly lit room. She overcame the battle within her to relocate Richard and his family based on Dr. Craig's instruction. She did everything to avoid his mother but she failed as the older woman sought her out and gave her the warmest hug she ever had in appreciation of everything she had done for her son. Whispering amid the chattering at the background, she told Hadiza, "Tonight, I will tell my son everything... I mean everything. The earlier he knows, the best for everyone. I can no longer keep up with the deception..." Hadiza nodded lamely, and stood up to leave. She stopped to give Richard an affectionate hug and informed him she would be traveling out of the country on a short course she had held down because of his accident - she would be away for three weeks. Richard confused by the suddenness of the information inquired if all was well; he could see the sadness in her eyes and suspected that something about this sudden trip did not fit. He composed himself, promising to call her the next day to discuss further on the trip.

There was no planned course for Hadiza; she wanted to get

away. Richard's mother decision to disclose 'everything' to her son that night was destabilizing. She had hoped that the 'lie' would continue for a longer time; however, she understood Richard's mother's intentions were good because she loved her son very much. She could not stand his rejection but could live with her parents' anger – and possible 'excommunication'. As she drove home, she decided to inform her parents about the events of the last one-month drama – the lies must stop! It was better coming from her because Dr. Craig could inadvertently tell her uncle, who would definitely inform his brother, her father. Hadiza also knew she was playing with fire, knowing that her father was a tough nut to crack; in spite of his love for her, Hadiza knew that her father would be very disappointed. On her way home, she decided to stop by Aunt, Aishat to sound her out – her Aunt was her father's favourite sibling.

Aunt Aishat, a widow, studied in one of United Kingdom's most prestigious university; a very successful Architect, and detribalized, she has clients from across the globe. Since her husband's death in a traffic air crash, Aunt Aishat had focused on her career and training her two sons. While her husband was alive, she built her business and determined to be self-reliant. Thus, when her husband died, she left her financial entitlements as the first wife to her co-wives who had no means of sustenance. Periodically, she supports her co-wives and, where necessary, their children. At this time, Aunt Aishat needed my professional perspective in rebranding her company as well as improved performance across board. Having known her for almost half a decade, we had worked business integrity and compliance matrixes over time. We had been working for about four hours in her study when the door opened and Hadiza ran in, sat down and sobbed. Aunt Aishat looked at me questioningly; I could only shake my head in consternation. What could have broken Hadiza down this way?

Hadiza was allowed to cry her heart out as we watched in silence. She wept like someone who had lost someone dear to her; no one interrupted this emotional display. Aunt Aishat moved closer to her and inquired about her parents were okay; Hadiza nodded in between sobs. She told herself that she needed to unclutter her head; she had to tell her Aunt who is very understanding. Taking the box of tissues offered by her Aunt, Hadiza dropped the ball, "I married a dying man to enable the doctors treat him; I was his security for the surgeries and treatments. I love him but he is poor and not of our religion – you know my parents will not hear of it. Now I am on the verge of losing him. I am fighting on all fonts, Auntie – My parents, Richard and his mother… What has class got to do with love? I am so confused, I don't know what to do…" Hadiza said, the tears streaming down her cheeks.

Aunt Aishat and I exchanged glances in a silence that was disturbing; she was very anxious about what the problem was with her niece. Having been assured that her brother and his family is okay, she needed clarity on the strange Hadiza 'married – who was the 'dying man'… We allowed her to cry her heart out; tears are sometime therapeutic as venting mechanism. Hadiza had been carrying a lot of emotional baggage, and it was time to let it go. After what seemed like ages passed, Aunt Aishat could no longer hold her peace, "Nellie, do you understand what Hadiza is talking about? Who is this dying man? When was the marriage organized? I got not invitations – and, I should be the one organizing my niece's wedding. What is really going on?"

One cardinal rule in managing emotional problems is the need to strict confidentiality – and there was no way I would tell Aunt Aisha the tons of emotional burden that Hadiza had had to cope with these past months. I had advised Hadiza on the need to consult someone she could trust within the family, but she believed that the time was not right. Hadiza wanted Richard to be released from the hospital; she had struggled to keep everything under radar and acted variety of scripts at home. Hadiza had the confidence of both parents – so none of them suspected that their only daughter was experiencing emotional somersaults and distress. What we were witnessing was the boiling point of bottled emotions – now the lid was off and vapours are escaping with a velocity that could not be controlled. Devastated by the sight of an emotionally wrangled Hadiza, I knew she needed to be encouraged to open up. Rising from my seat close to the flip chart I had been writing potential strategies for rebranding, I took her hands and squeezed gently, "'Diza, we have come full circle and need to face the issues at hand. We want to help you, however, only you can explain things to Aunt Aishat. You have done well to come here at this time; to face your parents, you ought to have all the answers. We are here to help, please trust your Aunt…"

Hadiza slowly took Aunt Aishat through the last 18 months of her life filled with apprehensions and unfulfilled emotions – a period characterized by fear, anger, despair and dejection.

For 18 months her life had been on a crossroad without a compass that would take her to her desired destination. After the narration, she turned to her Aunt "Auntie, please tell me what 'social class' has to do with who you fall in love with. I love my religion, but I don't want to be married with the knowledge that I will share my husband some day… I love Richard but his mother constantly reminds me of the 'Class and Religious difference'. So far, Richard and I respect each other's religious belief. Marrying him was in desperation to save his life. Tonight, his mother will tell him all that took place – the 'emergency wedding' and the hospital bills. I don't know how he will take all these. I cannot lose him because I love him very much…. Please help me."

Hadiza's Aunt called her brother to inform him that Hadiza was at her home; she knew it was going to be a long night. After nearly three hours of dissecting and analytically reasoning all possible angles, Aunt Aishat and I agreed that Hadiza needed a good rest. It was important not to jump the gun – Hadiza needed to hear from Richard before 'hurting' herself further. It was foolhardy to untangle the web without his input – Richard may be willing to fight for their love – regardless of class and religion. Richard could also decide to validate the 'emergency wedding', which could present another route in resolving her emotional confusion. Well aware that her father was very influential in the country, Hadiza also feared for Richard's safety. On many occasions, her father had arranged to marry her off to sons of his business partners from the same 'social class and religion', but Hadiza had resisted the moves – determined to marry on her own terms. With her emotions were in disarray – sleep was miles away for everyone because of Hadiza's circuitous emotional reality.

Lying down in the guest room of Aunt Aishat's palatial home, I could not help but be concerned about how these twists in the fate of two people that obviously love each other would be resolved. The greatest challenge was how Aunt Aishat would engage her brother…what strategy would she deploy. At the light tap on the door, I was startled, returning from my valleys of depressive analyses. Aunt Aishat was at the door; "My dear, Hadiza's problem has taken away our sleep. How do we help my niece? It is strange that we work so hard to give our children the best in life but they choose something extremely different from our desires for them. My brother is a tough nut to crack; he might end up disowning Hadiza if things are not carefully handled." She handed me a glass of fresh lemon juice on ice. "I know you have been thinking…can you share your thoughts with me… this is going to be a long night." Predictably, it was because we stayed up all night analyzing different possibilities and scenarios – including strategies for engaging Hadiza's father. Exhausted, we agreed to take at break at 4:00a.m.

Hours later, the smell of my favourite coffee, followed by the opening of the door woke me; Aunt Aisha sat at the edge of the bed, "Time to solve the puzzle girl – the final piece of the puzzle is here…Richard is in the sitting room." She handed the cup and left the room; I had a brief quiet time and freshened up for the parley ahead of us. Richard was the independent variable in the drama; upon his decision rests the happiness of a sweet young, selfless and impulsive 'wife'. Would he want to remain married, or has his mother convinced him that 'class and religious differences' far outweigh true love as exhibited by Hadiza? Would his 'poverty pride' deny him of a role model wife? These questions continued circuitously as I made haste to join the trio already seated. Richard had bags under his eyes like the rest of us – indicative of a long and restless night – but looking decisive. The lovebirds sat in silence without speaking to each other as the tension in the room reached its peak. Taking my seat, I attempted to diffuse the obviously unfriendly air. "Whose burial are we about to plan? The three of you look like someone died…Haba!" The duo seemed to relax a little but Aunt Aishat looked proudly offended wondering what this 'classless boy' had that made her niece. However, she gave me a look indicative that we needed to get this discussion over with.

Richard was on edge and felt like someone in the courtroom standing trial for a crime that could earn him a death sentence. He had called Hadiza repeatedly all night to speak with her after his mother told him the truth about everything that had happened during his 18 days in coma and subsequent bills offset by Hadiza. She further revealed that Hadiza loved him, but she had told Hadiza that the relationship could not be considered because of the major 'divide' between them. Hadiza gave him details of where she was and he'd come over to discuss 'face to face'. The situation did not call to rigmarole, so I was straight to the point, after general pleasantries and asking about his health. "Richard, you are the missing part in the puzzle. Having heard from your mother, it would be helpful to have your honest perspective. First, I need to ask a foundational question upon which every other discussion here is predicated, 'Do you love Hadiza'? I want certainty, not wishful thinking." Richard gave an equivocal "Yes". I continued, "Good. Now, how do you respond to the issues around your relationship with Hadiza?" When Richard began to speak, it became clear to Aunt Aishat why her niece had fallen hopelessly in love with him. He spoke with gusto, respect, confidence and assurance.

"I love 'Diza and she knows it. Before now we had talked about the differences between us – Tribe, Class and Religion. This demonic triangle had held me down. I come from a very poor background, but we are honest and hardworking people. My father died when I completed by primary education; so my illiterate mother, a petty trader, had struggled to train the three of us. As the eldest, she concentrated on training me with the hope that I would support her in training my brother and sister. God brought Hadiza to brighten my life – she may not be aware that I have become a better person and seen life from different lenses since we met about two years ago. I never thought that she felt anything deeper for me than friendship; her friendship is awe inspiring, thus, I never at-tempted anything emotional that could taint the cordiality and honest friendship we share. What can I offer 'Diza? How would I maintain her Class? Would I ask her to convert to Christianity when she is perfect in her religion? Would I offer her a low-class neighbourhood in exchange for the elitist and reserved neighbourhood? Can I afford to buy or maintain the cars she has? I am a man with dignity; I have often told her that I am afraid of deep emotional engagement because be-tween us stand the Mediterranean and Red Seas. How can we navigate through these obstacles that seem easy, but complicated? How would her family perceive me? Definitely, a 'gold digger' and opportunist'.

"Listening to my Mom yesterday as she relayed all the events that took place when I was practically a dead man, I could not help but see God's hand; in taking the greatest risk in life, 'Diza inadvertently propelled us to the path we are meant to be. How can you not holistically love the woman that married you when you had five percent chance of living in order to save the same life that was labeled 'dead'? I owe my life to her. How could my mother or anyone think that I would annul the most important event in my life – my marriage to 'Diza? My accident was divine – intended to open my eyes to the fact that everything is possible if God's Hands are in it. I know that this is the case here. One thing I can promise today is that I will never take advantage of her love – I will be 100% faithful because she is the breath that I take; I pledge to return the life that she gave me back to her…" Looking up from my electronic notepad, I could see the tears coursing through the cheeks of all in the room. Richard's response was touching.

Rising from her seat with tears still streaming down, Aunt Aishat walked to where the young man was sitting, pulled him up and gave him a warm but powerful hug. They stayed entwined for an immeasurable time before she broke off, reaching out Hadiza, she said, "Nellie and I did not have a night, but your speech has made up for the 'sleep fast'. We could not make any sensible conclusion without hearing from you, Richard. God is fixing things, but I must warn that this journey is going to be torturous. My brother is not an easy man – and not easily swayed by fancy words; he wants facts and balance sheets. However, if God stepped ahead of us and made my niece commit to a dying man, then, He must find a way out." She sat between Richard and Hadiza, probing further: "How would you children handle the religious difference?" Silence pervaded, but Richard turned to Hadiza, held her hands and spoke gently, "There is no pressure. If her religion taught her to be selfless, sacrificial, loving and faithful, there is no need to 'change' her. We are mostly a product of our upbringing; Muslim or Christian, a good marriage is predicated on how people relate - by respecting each others' strengths, weaknesses and idiosyncrasies – because we all have different background and exposure. I trust God will help us work things our as we cannot afford to mess up." Richard concluded.

Aunt Aishat called all to the dining table where everyone ate in pregnable silence. She interrupted private thoughts with a stupefying decision, "This afternoon, I will enter the 'lion's den' to speak to your father about everything after consulting with my lawyers... No doubt, the marriage is legal, but someone may punch hole on the 'manner'. I know that as long as both of you want to stay married, it is difficult to question because both of you are adults and in sound mind...I don't know how your father will react to the knowledge that his only daughter married about a month ago – and organized an 'emergency wedding'! I need the e-copy of the marriage certificate and pictures. Your parents need to understand this actually happened. It will be disastrous if journalists get to them first... you can imagine the headlines... That will kill your father who already has a heart condition... It will be better he hears from me than from Drs. Craig and Mohammed. This 'tiny thing' can snowball into a major disaster…"

The next couple of weeks were trying for the couple; Hadiza's father did not giving in and was ready to 'finish' Richard. He accused him of voodoo, claiming that his daughter had been conned into a 'sham' marriage because Richard's family had cast a spell on his daughter. 'What covenant has my daughter with poverty? I brought the best men she could marry, but she was rude enough to tell me she would not marry into the religion because of the potential for polygamy…We are Africans, and a man can marry as many women as he can love and care for. The best insurance has always been marrying into a wealthy family – then you are sure that you can be well catered for… what is wrong with my daughter?' he pondered repeatedly. He was disappointed in his sister, Aishat with all her emotional talk; money is determines emotional stability and disregarding the religion they had been borne into, which has been instrumental in prominent business opportunities. 'What is love when the pocket is empty? He wondered. The more he thought about his daughter's 'stupidity', the angrier he got. He concluded that his daughter's behaviour was disgraceful; the best was to cut her off. He was convinced that the threat of cutting her off would bring his daughter 'back to her senses'.

Hadiza expected her father's anger – and decision to cut her off. She was determined to preserve what she had with Richard and took steps to secure their future. She knew her father's love and support were critical to her overall happiness, but was not ready to jettison her life to salvage the 'family honour' – whatever that was. She believed that the most important thing in life is to follow your heart and watch how your mind is mutilated. They were at a major crossroad that would test their love; Richard had to leave her father's bank before he was fired which would make it challenging to get another job. She found him a job in a reputable Investment Company that had managed her funds for over a decade and registered a joint Auditing Firm, with Richard as the CEO - provide outsourced auditing support to her company. She knew Richard's competence as Forensic Accountant and Auditor - and how he had helped her resolve some thorny issues for which specialist firms charge millions of Naira. In her position as a Senior Vice President in an International Auditing Company where she worked, Hadiza used her influence to encourage company consultant to throw things Richard's way to enable them make money on the side. For integrity and clarity, Richard officially documented his interest in the 'family business' to Investment Company where he worked and got required legal approvals.

With Hadiza moving in with Aunt Aishat, the couple were forced to live apart, but maximized every opportunity they had together. Aunt Aishat became convinced that Richard was genuine; their love was indeed worth fighting for. Aunt Aisha had wondered why Hadiza had not paid for an apartment and moved in with her 'husband' was impressed that Richard wanted to save up for the rent. They had perfected plans to get Richard's mother and siblings to live with them at the first instance, and later get a smaller apartment for Richard's family. Richard had been working tirelessly to ensure he saved for the house; he stayed with Aunt Aishat and Hadiza from Friday till Monday. Aunt Aishat observed that the logistics implications of this lifestyle was affecting Richard's health, but be refused to move in with his 'favourite and supportive' in-law – placing the resolution of the accommodation challenge as critical. His mother had come to accept Hadiza except she wanted to 'lose' her son. He could see the visible maturity of her son as he worked determinedly to achieve certain set goals – and prayed for him constantly.

Six months on… on a sunny Saturday, Aunt Hadiza observed something 'strange' about her niece; she was looking pale as she worked with her on the sofa. She interrupted Hadiza's work, asking her if she was doing okay. Hadiza answered in the affirmative, but her Aunt prodded further, worried that the situation with her brother was causing her to lose weight and not eat well. Recently she observed that her niece had not been sleeping well, too. As Hadiza attempted to rise, she staggered, but her aunt caught her before she could fall. "Hadiza, I think you need to check your glucose level hypoglycemia is very dangerous." Before Hadiza could protest, her aunt called in the family doctor to 'look her over'. Dr. Hamid, who had his Clinic less than 10 minutes drive from Aunt Aishat's residence, responded promptly. Aunt Aishat was present during the examination; dissatisfied with the check, Dr. Hamid requested Hadiza stop by the Clinic. Alarmed, Aunt Aishat complied and waited at the reception. After about 30 minutes, Aunt Aishat was called in and informed that Hadiza was pregnant; she received the news with mixed feelings worried about her brother who had refused to speak with neither his daughter nor sister. How would her brother take the news that his daughter is pregnant for 'her nonentity husband' (as her brother always described

Richard?)? Hadiza was very excited and called Richard immediately to inform him that he would soon be a father.

Richard rushed back home from the office where he had gone to finish some outstanding work left the previous day. As he boarded a taxi home, he told himself of two critical items – an apartment and a car. He needed to speak with Human Resources the next working day to explore the possibility of a loan to enable him save Hadiza from further ridicule and embarrassment by his family. Aunt Aishat had been the only support from Hadiza's family and often wondered how things would have been if her parents had understood that they loved each other and accepted their relationship. Now he was going to be a father; his mother was excited that she would be a grandmother soon – still concerned about Hadiza's parents. Despite the dampening thoughts of her brother, Aunt Aishat was happy for the couple because a baby changes the landscape and Hadiza needed something to distract her from thinking about her parents. She loved them, but could not understand why they would not surrender any ground for the happiness of their daughter. She had no regrets about her love for Richard; his mother and siblings had surprised her by the warmth and understanding she received. His sister, the most outspoken of the children, told her mother they would leave her to live with Auntie Hadiza if she does not accept her as her daughter. Hadiza felt loved and cared for; Richard's mother called her daily to encourage, strengthen and pray with her. There was no harm in 'Amen' when someone blesses you and asks God to protect you… the prayers also made her realize that beyond the strict countenance was a very soft and warmhearted woman.

During the week after her pregnancy announcement, Richard got multiple URGENT 'financial investigation' contracts. He checked into a nearby hotel so that he could maximize after work hours to work on the contracts. He also sought the support of the other 'Fast Five' members, who were excited at any opportunity to make 'extra hustling dough'. Payments were prompt on work completion; Richard was grateful to God because through the jobs, they now had enough money for a two-year rent, a fairly used SUV in perfect condition and savings. Hadiza was tasked to look for the house of their choice within budget; she was happy that Richard had not disappointed her by venturing into unnecessary expense, making mental note to change his wardrobe. With the help of Aunt Aishat, they got a fully furnished house belong to Aunt Aishat's friend who was relocating abroad; the family had wanted to dispose of their household items and put the house on lease. Aunt Aishat intervened and sealed the deal on the property. Arrangement for assessment of the household items was completed including payment plan; Aunt Aishat was happy to facilitate everything so that her niece could settle down and run her home independently. She gave Hadiza two of her domestic staff to help the young family settle in with little stress.

Months went by and Hadiza was safely delivered of twin boys; Aunt Aishat independently organized for Islamic rights to be conducted in her house for the boys without the boys being physically present, while Richard's mother planned for a Child Dedication program. They were bundles of joy for her and a fulfillment of God's promise that His Children would live to see their grandchildren. As Aunt Aishat feted his friends in celebration of the new addition, her brother walked and gave her a hug that spoke volumes, "Sister, I have been foolish; ninety percent of my boards are made of Christians and we have been working together without integrity breach all these years. I have denied myself the love of a daughter who loves me very much – and is twice as stubborn. While, she lived a fulfilled life, I have driven myself poorly and my health is deteriorating fast due to anger. I also shut you out, my favourite sibling... how foolish. No one can tell a bird where to perch – the same way we cannot direct the heart who to love. When Dr. Craig gave me the details of the case, I shuddered because our daughter made me proud. I was taken round the hospital as the father of 'angel Hadiza' who organized that 'emergency wedding' to save a man that had less than 10% chance of surviving. Please take me to see my grandsons and their parents. One of them must be named after me..."

One hour later, Hadiza got the greatest surprise of her life as her Aunt came in with her parents; they held her in warm embrace on the bed because due to the surgery, she was advised to minimize movements. Richard and his parents stood by to watch the emotional expression, unsure of what to expect. He wondered why Aunt Aishat did not warn them of his parents-in-law's visit to enable them adequately prepare for the visit. Hadiza's father turned to Richard, "My son, please forgive the sentiments and folly of a 'Medieval Boardroom Guru'; come and give me a well-deserved hug for transforming my daughter with your love..." Hadiza's mother walked to Richard's mother – the two women were locked for a long time in emotions and tears overflowing in the wells of apology. That day the Mediterranean and Red Sea merged into one endless nameless Atlantic an expression of the powerful influence of the love that overcame Class and Religion Clashes.

Emotional Piggy Bank

Class and Religious barriers are every day realities. In a relationship, the barriers are further magnified – deliberately or inadvertently. Couples always believe in the old saying that "love conquers all", unfortunately little or no attempts are made to deal with the 'present or distant danger' to relationships. Class and religious differences create expectations – sometimes good and other times, bad for relationships. Dealing with these realities requires positive action steps in accepting each partner's strengths and supporting areas needing improvement.

Where emotions and love are concerned, the heart is unable to determine the 'Class' or 'Religion' of who to fall in love with. Our hearts remain fixated on the subject of our love, influencing the emotions to live in alignment with its thoughts and yearnings. Whenever there is a 'class clash' or religious irreconcilable differences, mutual respect remains the stabilizing factor the ferries the couple across troubled waters. Since we are relational beings, thoughts and actions must put external factors into consideration – to integrate, align and reason. Communication, fidelity and rationality are key ingredients in sustaining a harmonious and long lasting relationship.

Of Class Clash or Religious Divide – the heart remains ignorant!

7

Episode 7

Emotional Blackmail or Love?
...Save Me from Mutual Polygamy

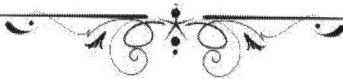

Every relationship is complex, although each couple experience complexities in a diverse fashion. Growing up, my parents were the model couple – they never exchanged words of bitterness or anger. They loved different sports – yet agreed on the basics of sporting – respecting each other's views on issues. On the other hand, my primary school classmates in school gave terrifying accounts of the 'war' in their homes – stories ranged from fights, verbal and physical abuses, hospitalization – the full works. Looking back, you could see they spoke with innocence, unaware of the import of each detail in their stories. Their stories were always exciting because they share the information with so much passion as if recalling scenes from a horror movie, because a 'Voltron-like' figure always saved the helpless character from being 'extinguished'. Sometimes, I felt uncomfortable or ashamed because there were not excitements in my home; I had to ask my dear mother, "How come you and dad don't fight?" I asked with the petulance of a child. "It is because you cannot fight yourself", she said absent-mindedly.

As I grew older, I understood my mother's decades-old answer, which has remained the philosophical foundation for me in any relationship: You cannot fight yourself! Unfortunately, since many people enter into relationships with unrealistic grounding, things gradually fall apart. This explains lack of emotional elasticity among friends, lovers, partners and spouses. Scriptural or Divine Mathematics buttresses the principle of ONENESS in spousal bonding – "…and the two shall become one". When we fight or betray someone we are emotionally or spiritually bound to, we hurt ourselves. Every relationship is a TRUST – a repository of the entirety of our spiritual, emotional, physical, financial treasures, for which a breach can be life threatening. However, since God created us in His Image and deposited in us an "Inner Resilience" called "the Spirit man", whenever we are at the end of our tethers, "Help" comes from within to connect with the external – propelling us from the submarine called dejection.

It is the 'Power Within' that helps us handle the disappointments we face arising from a breach of trust. Whenever any component within the Trust-bond is breached, every deposits in the repository is compromised – "things fall apart and the center cannot hold" – as Africa's Literary Legend, Chinua Achebe puts it. It is important to state that having achieved adulthood, these foundational lessons become very portent; these form the bases for determining the 'Ideal man' and 'Ideal woman' from an individual perspective. Couples walk the aisle when they are convinced that their partners have demonstrated emotional and trust connection that align with individual relationship principles. These principles are expected to be the binding wires that ensure relationship longevity. While these seem to have worked for many, for some, their dreams crumble like a pack of cards as it was with Anne.

Anne called in to my live radio talk show "Emotionally Yours" to express her disappointment in her husband of 18 years, who had decided to fill Anne's 'gap' as a wife with another wife in what he called, Mutual Polygamy. Devastated by her husband's insensitivity, Anne approached us for guidance – she needed to explore ways of keeping her marriage, but uncomfortable with her husband's strategy for both women to live 'happily ever after' in the same house. Listening to Anne at the radio station, everyone in the studio was impacted by her emotion-laden voice. Undeniably broken, Anne had a positively compromising plan to win back her husband by allowing his whim – clearly reaching out for someone out there to support her. The telephone lines did not stop as callers gave their perspectives – it was indeed a mixed grill.

Stepping out of the station, I called Anne and had a long discussion with her to get deeper insights into the real issues (airtime does not give you all the time to need to probe). Anne offered to provide additional clarity on what she called a 'betrayal of faith, emotion and trust'. Interestingly, when Anne wrote to Emotionally Yours, it was without sentiments as she struggled to revive her marriage and rescue her husband from "the other woman" who had captured the only man she ever loved. She was ready to compromise, regardless the obvious humiliation as expressed in her treatise below:

*"My name is Anne. I have been married for 18 years. I am a banker and my husband, Fred, is a businessman. We are blessed with two wonderful children. My son is 10 years old, while my daughter is 13. About three months ago, Fred at last confessed that he has found and fallen in love with a "wife material". According to him, they met about 18 months ago on 3rd Mainland Bridge on his way from work when he assisted this 'lonely lady' with a flat tyre. As a matter of fact, I recall that he came home usually late that day and explained how he played the 'Good Samaritan' to a 'distressed lady'. Little did I know that that chance meeting and the Good Samaritan role would impact our marriage negatively.... He suggests **"Mutual Polygamy"** which would mean my accepting Gloria, his mistress as my 'co-wife' and living together "in holy matrimony"... Really Weird!!!*

*My husband has pledged his 'undying love' to Gloria – claiming he loves both of us equally! I really do not know where **"Mutual Polygamy"** came from – maybe it was created to address the emotional and confidence crisis that best* *describes our marriage. According to Fred, he loves me and cannot give me up; nor would he give up his relationship with this **"Angel of my Dream"**. Fred constantly praises her work, intelligence, sound business judgment – even celebrates Gloria's major business breakthroughs at home. However, Fred has never allowed the relationship with Gloria affect the children in any way, insisting that I should not inform the children about the developments in our home. They are still ignorant that Daddy has a bride in waiting ...*

"

My husband has remained very attentive - even more caring since he revealed his 'mutual polygamy plan' to me. For me, these last three months have been filled with emotional stress and mental agony – very traumatizing! However, Fred carries on without any cares – as if all is well...I begin to wish he never told me about Gloria. He said he had to tell me because we agreed never to hide anything from each other – how cruel.

"Last week, I went to see his eldest sister for advice. Auntie Christy, 56, was very calm and listened to me empathically. She submitted that Fred already told her about Gloria, but had advised her brother to quit the relationship. However, when she noticed Fred's firm resolve, she told him I deserved to know if he is determined to get another wife. Traditionally, my consent would be required for Fred to get another wife 'officially'. Aunty Christy said she could not advise me because she loves Fred and I equally. She would not want to be in the middle of this 'messy conflict'.

Auntie Jane, Christy's friend, who listened to our discus-

*sions, asked what I really wanted; I was transfixed with con-
fusion. She spoke candidly: "Anne, mutual polygamy means
you will accept Gloria as your husband's wife and be willing
to progress marital rites with your husband. You will vow to
live happily as mature adults (like our mothers loved and
shared the love of one man in ancient times). The other
choice is to allow Fred to marry Gloria and seek divorce.
Young lady, these are hard choices to make...You need to retreat and seek spiritual help or professional counsel."*

*I am in dire straits because I love my family; Fred and I
have known each other all our lives - from Secondary School
through University education till date. He is the only man I
have ever known and still love. Above all, despite his betrayal, I still love Fred; I cannot live without him, however, I
agree with him on 'mutual polygamy'... It is frustrating. I
cannot share his love and cannot endure living under the
same roof with a co-wife and my children. How do I tell my
children that their father would bring another wife home?*

*Recently, I have been feeling suicidal, but the thought of
my children constrained me from such devilish thought...I
need help NOW! Please help me.*
                    --ANNE

Reading Anne's letter brought back my early years; I
thought of what I would have said to my mother if she informed me that my father would be bringing home another
wife – whom he loved so much? I also thought of how my
mother would have reacted to that situation. I imagined how
the home would be for my father, because my mother loved

my father to the point of near obsession. Would we still sing hymns on Preparation Day or walk together to Church on Sabbath Day? Would my mother still sing joyful praises in the Choir – or me, with the Children's Choir? Furthermore, I close my eyes to our joyful home then, and imagined what Morning and Night Prayers would look like. Would the 'new addition be scheduled to say the Word and Prayer 'for the Family? Oh, No…Without a shadow of doubt, the home would have been a decided 'HELL' for everyone – my parents and all of us. If my dear mother had been in Anne's shoes, how would she tackle my father?

One of the lessons during my formative years is almost eternally enduring: *FIGHTING OR MISTREATING THE ONE YOU LOVE IS INFLICTING EMOTIONAL WOUNDS ON YOUR CONSCIENCE!* This explained Fred's inability to face his children with the 'truth' about his new found 'wife material'. Innately, we know when we hurt someone, especially, anyone with who we are emotionally connected – no matter how brief. Thus, Fred too, was struggling with a 'monster' too big to contain, hence, his admission that he was 'in love' with another woman, besides Anne. I am not one who believes that the relationship suddenly went downhill; something must have driven Fred – rightly or wrongly – to seek solace in the arms of another woman. As women, we are often encapsulated in our personal points of view, while staying deaf to the yearnings of our partners. Farmers know that the seed germination does not happen overnight – it takes nurturing; we also inadvertently provide the fertilizer that fast tracks unfaithfulness, driving our partners into the arms of other women – or friends with destructive habit. Of course, many men CHOOSE that path in spite of having 'The World Best' wife/partner. In spite of how the actions hurt, 'Conscience', indeed, is an open wound requiring truth to heal.

If Fred was not willing for his children to know about a 'second mother', he was not proud of himself. However, a meeting with him provided deeper insight that numbs every knife of anger emanating from Anne's emotion-laden letter. Fred, a man of few words felt uneasy about what felt like being put on the dock; he displayed candour and desire to resolve the dark cloud that was robbing him and Anne of happiness in the recent months...

"Let me start by stating that I am not proud of what I have done; unfortunately, there is nothing I can do about it because I love both women. Women often see things from myopic lenses; they do not always take in the whole picture. What the world knows today is that I have decided to abandon my wife of over 18 years – no one is interested in how I have survived the last eight years. I am from a solid family background, where the woman welds the broken pieces to ensure her family is intact. My wife is not perfect – neither am I; the bond of marriage requires the stronger to support the weaker. My wife is an excellent banker and financial risk manager, who has worked various financial and investment institution. I have done my best to ensure that she is not distracted from the course of her career. I love my wife very much.

"It is important to state that I did not wake up one day to take a second wife – everything happened as if ordained by God Himself. During the past 18 years, I have had over two-dozen domestic staff – out of which we've had a new cook every year. Anne is very career focused and we have enjoyed the dividends as a family. She has played major roles in placing our family among the privileged rank in this country – for this, I am eternally grateful. Every man desires a wife like my wife, who would contribute positively to the home; of course, with this comes some domestic challenges. Gloria is a businesswoman with control of her time and schedule; her husband died in a plane crash leaving her alone with her a 9-year-old son. I saw a courageous young woman changing a flat tyre at about 2300 hours, on one on the most dangerous bridges in the country – the Third Mainland Bridge. I was drawn by something stronger than my commonsense to stop because it could have been a set up. It was raining and nobody wanted to risk stopping to help someone who could be part of a robbery gang. Gloria genuinely needed help, and by Divine intervention, I was there to help.

"Over the weeks that followed, I found we shared the same interests in business – telecommunications. Gloria is an Electrical/Electronic Engineer with impressive professional certifications that dwarfs the best of men; yet, she is humble as she is homely. I was fascinated by her maturity and ability to combine motherhood and business without the other suffering. Gradually, we grew inseparable without any physical contact, no sex. I had fallen in love with her, but I was also afraid that sex could ruin the relationship. I began spending more time with her – appreciating the firm but loving manner she handled her son. At 10 Gloria's son was already a gentleman who could do chores and fix uncomplicated meals for his mother. Unfortunately, I began to compare my home with

Gloria's, trying to see what module I could transfer home for implementation. My home is not perfect, but it has served me. It is inevitable that when you are with a woman (even those who you do not have emotional commitment to), there is a natural tendency to compare. I made efforts to my wife to visit Gloria with me; my intention was for Anne to appreciate how Gloria is able to joggle the balls and still create quality time for her son. My wife rebuffed me, saying I indirectly wanted to take her to my mistress.

"I have an open marriage – with no secrets at all. My wife shares problems with the opposite sex at work and I always supported her by providing insights as a man. I taught her how to handle sexual harassments and intimidations. Naturally, I discussed Gloria at every opportunity I met with or spoke with Gloria. After some months passed, I invited Gloria to my home after Sunday Service. She was happy to meet my wife; we watched an interesting thriller in the living room, while the children had fun upstairs, engaging in different activities. The two women connect just like the children. Subsequently, my children pleaded for Gloria's son to spend some weekends with them, which was welcomed by my wife. My wife did not miss the connection the children had; seeing them together, you would believe that they are siblings. My wife and Gloria later developed a friendship with Gloria, encouraging her to drop off her son with us whenever she had business meetings outside the state. I loved the relationship between the two women; Gloria's industry and ability to balance her business with quality time with her son was admirable. No matter how busy she was, she cooked, cleaned and washed – in addition to reviewing her son's homework.

She created time.

"My wife invited her to spend one of those long weekend holidays with us; although I felt some discomfort about it, to my greatest surprise, Gloria accepted. My wife and I had planned to spend that particular weekend at Abuja; that added to my confusion and worry. It turned out to be the most enjoyable time I ever spend with at home; Gloria took over the kitchen and made a variety of dishes to the excitement of my children. The children drew up continental-based menu table from Friday to Tuesday afternoon; my protest fell on deaf ears. Gloria was excited 'feeding' everyone, but I was concerned that she could be embarrassed. She did not disappoint us; the meals were excellent – from breakfast through supper! The impressionable thing was that she handled everything effortlessly, while Anne busied herself with office work. I was very disappointed by my wife's actions because she treated Gloria as if she was a mere maid who had been hired to cook for the weekend.

"There is something about the innocence of children – they tell speak the truth regardless of whose ox is gored. My children praised her cooking and talked about every dish at the dinning area and were excited about washing plates and cleaning the kitchen with her. She taught my daughter how to make her favourite pancake and scrambled eggs. She was very excited to try it all alone and Gloria 'forced' everyone to eat what my daughter cooked – irrespective of how it tasted. Oh, my God! My daughter had never entered the kitchen all her life because my wife ensured we have maids to do everything. Gloria brought excitement to our home and the children loved her even more. At the end of that long weekend I knew I was gradually falling in love with her; Gloria carried a positive spirit that charged any environment. The children called her often and the bond between the children grew stronger; she was a natural mother as she was able to deal with their 'questions' with the calmness of 'Mother Theresa'.

"As the weeks went by, I knew that my marriage was no longer exciting and took a personal retreat to establish the point of disconnection. I am aware that it is wrong to compare two women, however, there are basic expectations Motherhood entails which is clearly missing in my marriage. I blame myself for a lot of gaps today because I loved Anne to much to complain – her inability to cook, zero patience with the children and general lack of interest on how the home is run. I had tried to bridge the gap when the children were toddlers, but I cannot perpetually churn out maids to nurture my children. I had complained about her inability to 'create' time for the family; it would always turn into a theatre of war. My family is aware, but I try to shield her from direct affront by my family. It is my responsibility to protect my wife from verbal assault from my mother and sister in particular, but I needed her help by seeing her make a step change. Each time I raised the issue, she asked if the maid is incompetent and would swiftly change the staff the next day. My sister, I cannot continue this way…

"Few months ago, Anne needed to attend a three-week international training in the United States. I panicked because she was aware I had finalized plans to travel to China for the Canton Fair for one week. We agreed that NOTHING would make both of us stay away from the home at the same time – not even for one night. I pleaded with her to join the batch for her program, which was scheduled the next quarter, but she was vehement in her refusal – and promised to plead with Gloria to oversee the home until she returned. She said Gloria had spent five days with us, so one week should not be a problem until I got back from my scheduled China trip. The children were excited on hearing Gloria and her son would stay with them for 'a whole week' and looked forward to the visit; they even made 'a laundry list' of what they would ask Gloria to do for them. Although I was truly uncomfortable about Anne's plan, there was little I could do to stop it after my wife convinced her; she accepted. Thus, it was with mixed emotions that Gloria came to spend time with us. She settled in a day before my trip; Gloria insisted on everyone joining me to the airport and volunteered to drive home after the farewells. I was overjoyed because it was the first time 'my family' was driving to the airport to bid me 'safe journey'. In the 18 years of our marriage, even before the children were born, Anne never drove me to the airport – or even joined me from work. So, the 'family trip' to the airport was refreshing to me – and I held onto the memory throughout my stay in China.

"While in Beijing, I yearned to return 'home' and relieve that 'family feeling I enjoyed during the trip to the airport. As fate would have it, I accomplished the set goals in four days and quickly changed my flight for o return home. For some reason, I resisted telling Gloria that I would be returning ahead of schedule; my business partner, Tunde, volunteered to pick me on arrival. Tunde had been skeptical of Gloria and believed she had an agenda; he wanted us to 'see the real Gloria', as he put it. He posited that, in spite of my early morning arrival, he would drive me to his house to rest and return home late at night to see if Gloria was 'acting up' or just being her self. According to Tunde, a graduate of Criminology, there is no perfect criminal; they would always have their guards down when no one is watching. He suggested that activate my CCTV mobile app to view my home. I disagreed on the use of the mobile app, but agreed to rest at his residence before going home after dark; I needed to convince myself that Gloria was real.

"In line with the plan, Tunde picked me up on arrival to his house and I went straight to bed after freshening up; he went to work and left me in the care of his loving wife. It was a long trip with all the connections, so I needed to rest in order not to appear before the children like a rag doll. Tunde retuned home at about 2000 hours, had a quick meal, and drove me home. A few meters to my home, Tunde asked that we stopped by a pub close to my residential compound; we sat in a dimly lit bar where I could see my well lit home. It was 2130 hours. We requested for a bottled of beer after the attendant came to us for the umpteenth time for our order. We listened to conversations of other people having a meal or some kind of soup on their tables. Suddenly, a woman known for notoriety in the area stood up and said in Pidgin English, "That Mr. Fred has gone through deliverance. The Pastor or Priest that delivered him must be very powerful. He is a very good man; unfortunately, he married a witch and believes Madam Anne is an angel. He worships her. She does not cook, wash or do any chores at home. What about his children? They don't even come close to a broomstick. Recently, his mother brought him a very good wife who takes care of the children…. Yesterday, we say his daughter actually doing chores…She washed her clothes!!! That Madam Glory is the best thing for that children…" The bar room was filled with laughter, jest and scorn. People bantered and joked about my family. Something interesting had happened…. Did Gloria make my daughter wash? That would be a first… I looked at Tunde and signaled him it was time to leave; the less than 30 minutes was pointing me to the way home. Suddenly, I felt like being at home; I needed to see children before they slept.

"I let myself in with my bunch of keys and walked straight to the bedroom that Anne and I had shared all these years. Something seemed to have changed; I put on the full light to see that the room had been cleaned and the bathroom was sparkling clean – with toiletries well laid out in beautiful order. I quietly took a shower, using a bucket and bowl in order not to attract any attention because everywhere was quiet. It was indeed strange that the children would be sleeping at 2200 hours; this house has indeed changed in five straight days. Changing into my pajamas, I tiptoed into the kitchen for a warm milk to help me sleep because I was on nerves after the pub. Even in the dark, you could see that the kitchen was sparkling clean; everything was in its place – better organized. Above the gas cooker, I could see a paper pasted on the lid; with the LED light from my phone, it read "CLEAN ME BEFORE YOU LEAVE". I smiled. I turned to get a glass from one of the cupboard, only to find a menu table and those responsible for cooking, washing dishes and cleaning. I was overwhelmed with emotion as I made my warm milk and went back to my room in order not to upset the sparkling kitchen. Lying down on the large family bed, I wondered if this was my home; how did Gloria do it? My room was so painstakingly organized that I just laid down – afraid to disorganize the room, including he bed upon which I laid.

"I woke up close to midday to an empty house. Stepping out of the room to the Living Room, through downstairs to the kitchen and dining area – everywhere was clean and organized. How did they do this? How did Gloria do this without a maid? I was determined to find out, and deepened on my cheery son to tell me. Later that that, at about 1600 hours, Gloria drove in with the children; I could hear my daughter who seemed to be in charge, directing the boys "Let us change quickly, take a shower and bat at the dinning table in 30 minutes. Mummy G, you have 30 minutes to get lunch ready…see you guys later…" The children were so happy that I was tempted to reveal that I was back. Somehow, I prayed to be discovered, as the 30 minutes seemed like five, because I could hear my daughter ordering the boys to the table. "Mummy G, you skipped breakfast, so you must east with us…Come…" I hear Gloria say, "Yes Ma'am". I was tempted to join the 'happy band' but 'focus' on purpose won the day. I walked to a convenient point where I could see them… What a picture! It was an awesome sight!!! I yearned to be with them; the unfortunate ring of my phone cellphone exposed me. It was a call from worried Tunde. The children know my ringtone and turned to the direction of the sound; in order not to startle them, I announced myself and was welcomed with all the excitement you can best imagine - and practically forced to the table for late lunch.

"My daughter with an air of authority took charge; when I said I needed to eat semovita and native soup, she asked Gloria to please 'rescue' her. Gloria took my daughter to the kitchen to prepare my meal. I was stunned when my daughter actually served me the traditional way. It was an emotional scene as she dished, filled my glass, and sat down to keep me company. It was strange that she had not asked one million questions about what I bought for them, but she sat there, asking about my trip and weather. "My daughter is now an adult", I screamed within as I ate the delicious meal that could only have been prepared by Gloria! After the meal, we all sat down in the living room to watch a play; behold it was my   son's turn to pick a 30-minutes cartoon video for all to view; after that it prayer and bedtime. He chose "Beauty and the Beast"; Gloria asked the reason for his choice and he replied with all innocence, "The beautiful girl always changes he beast. When I grow up, I ask God for a Beautiful Girl to change me". There was laughter and jesting as my daughter searched for the video for all to watch. The film was just gathering momentum, when Gloria shouted "Time Up"; Gloria's son switched off the television and we held hands and prayed. The children obediently went to their room; Gloria began to organize the sitting room.

"Watching her from the dinning area where she had ordered me to relocate, I wondered how she could be this organized. Nothing in the house was out of place when I stepped out my room after they had left – Gloria to her office, and the children to school. I tried to see Anne in her – but it wasn't working. The bathroom in the Master bedroom, which Anne and I have used for over a decade, was unbelievably sparkling clean – almost brand new. Our wardrobes were organized according to cloth type; it was an amazing sight. As Gloria completed her chores and about to retire for the night, I called her to the dinning table for a brief chat, "Gloria, take a little break; come sit with me for 10 minutes before you go to bed. Tell me, how have the children been treating you? I am concerned that they are not overtasking you…" She smiled and sat at the opposite seat, pouring herself a glass of water, "Nope. They are wonderful and resourceful children. Yes, they ask a lot of question – and only because they want to know so much. You need elastic patience to handle them; the moment you remember that we were once children and did the same thing, you will understand their desire to know more…"

"Gloria told me how they divided chores to ensure that they met up with their individual schedules – school and work. "We agreed to distribute the chores among ourselves: They developed a menu table, so the young lady makes breakfast, while boys do the dishes; they collectively clean the kitchen. She is in CHARGE – whatever she churns out, we eat 'thankfully. However, I am general overseer – so I supervise 'meal standards' and take care of the other things in the house. We have a timetable prepared by them – so, they lead, I follow. As general overseer, I have supervisory oversight – that is simple, right. It is basic human resource management; everyone has something to give…" I was surprised that my children would be interested in kitchen chores and wished to see that by morning. My daughter in charge of breakfast…that is interesting. I made poured myself a glass of red wine as I told her how successful my trip was. As a businesswoman, who was very familiar with the complexities of doing business with reputable Chinese firms, we discussed potential and imminent opportunities from the trip. She also gave me reliable contacts that can help follow up and fast track my consignment.

"I was impressed with her insight, wondering how she had managed to handle the challenges involved in importation and supply. Above all, I wondered if she had a man in her life – and how much help the gentleman was supporting her effort. Suddenly, the thought of another man made my heart to sink with jealousy; the man must be angry that she is spending time taking care of a family that was not hers. Has the man been visiting my home to see her? My stomach tightened with anger; I was boiling with internal rage. "Gloria, I hope your boyfriend will not kill us for kidnapping you?" I joked lightly, trying to allow the anger to reduce a notch within. She smile, rising from her seat, "I don't have a boyfriend… the only man in my life is my son, Daniel – and that is by choice." Her response sounded like a 'snap', and I quickly apologized for my careless and senseless remark. She quickly realized how she sounded and apologized, stating calmly, "My late husband was the best thing that happened to me. Like you and Anne, we grew up together and were committed to each other until his death. He took with him every emotion and left bereft of any. So, I mind my business and take care of the only fruit of that 'made-in-Heaven' relationship. So, I am not angry, but the question reminded me of my husband – Yes, he was loving and possessive. Rather than cause any man emotional stress, I CHOSE to stay this way…"

"Gloria spoke about how her husband's family had wanted her to marry someone from their family; her refusal led to untold hardship and eventual loss of job in the successful business she and her husband ran, leaving them penniless. She had to start her business from nothing with the support of friends. I sat there imagining what this beautiful woman been through and wished to hold her my arms and shoo off the pains and agony. We bade each other good night, and, with a perfunctory hug, I walked to my bedroom, which suddenly felt like a stadium. I could not sleep as I lay there reflecting everything that Gloria told me; she seemed to relax in his arms as he gave her a hug. It wasn't the first hug we've had, but somehow, this particular hug was very soothing – though I didn't plan it. The rustling of the children made me look at the bedside clock which indicated 0530 hours; having waited for almost 45 minutes, I walked to the balcony to see the two boys brushing dust out of Gloria's car interior with excitement, while Gloria washed the body with admirable dexterity. She thanked they boys, urging them to hurry for breakfast in 20 minutes and they disappeared. Feeling a third party was watching, Gloria looked up, on seeing me, she waved a greeting and returned to her task. To avoid making her uncomfortable, I went down to the living room and was queried by my son who was seated at the dinning area waiting for others to join, "Daddy, you missed the morning devotion. I read the Psalm 121. God is our Helper." Seeing the questioning frown on my face, my son continued, "We wake up at 0530, read the Bible and pray for 10 minutes, do our chores for 20 or 30 minutes. We come for breakfast at a quarter to 0700, eat for 15 or 20 minutes. We leave home at 15 or 20 past 7 o'clock to get to school on time. Today, Mummy G woke up late, so we helped her clean the car, while Crystal fixed the breakfast... It's been fun Dad..."

"Breakfast was fun as I watched my children eat with discipline that had not been there. There were no chatters or fights or arguments; there was courtesy, and when they finished eating, collectively, they tidied the table and off to the car. I felt like a stranger in my own home; my children were more respectful towards me, displayed a sense of purpose and respect for time. Gloria seemed to be bemused by the 'strange way' I looked at my children; as she walked to the door, I rose to meet her and gave her a tight hug with tear veiling my eyes. I could not speak, but felt grateful for the transformation I witnessed; the hug was broken by the blaring of the car horn, signally Gloria that it was time to go. I kissed her on the forehead to her shock and ran up the stairs to my bedroom in embarrassment as I realized that something stirred inside me. Lying down on my cold bed, I all kinds of thoughts ran through my head. Gloria is an epitome of motherhood; in five days, my children had undergone a major 'surgery' and all the negative manners seemed to have gone down the gutters. Even Anne would not recognize her children on return. I had not doubt that I wanted Gloria permanently in our lives.

"They came back early because it was a Friday. Gloria was her normal self as the children insisted on staying in her room for siesta. She handled every other chore with the precision of a habit that had become second nature. I later joined her in the living room where she was watching a feminine-type drama; we chatted and exchanged views on the drama. Impulsively I asked her views about polygamy; with equal petulance, she asked jokingly, "Fred, do you want to marry me?" I chuckled, "You know, it would be a fulfilling experience for me…. But you know, I am below your standard…" We bantered heartily for about an hour; Gloria was relaxed and was in a weekend spirit, ready to leave the next day. "Anyway, you know I will be leaving tomorrow – you are back ahead of time, which is good for me…" There was impregnable silence; even the voices from the television were like a distant sound. I began to imagine what my home would look like without Gloria – I would be back to cooking my own meals and patronizing restaurant again. The thought frightened me. Sitting with her in my living room felt so good and right; it felt like her natural place. I felt a sudden whiff of chill coursing through me at the thought of losing her. Since desperate situations require desperate strategy, I asked a stupid question that could only come from a teenager, "Gloria, don't you like me…love me?" Gloria was bemused and began to laugh; I held my gaze, unmoved by the laughter because I was very serious – irrespective of how stupid my question sounded.

"After what seemed like eternity, Gloria stopped laughing and said: "Fred, you are a good man; you also have a wonderful family and I love them – including Anne. Of course, I like you and everyone in your household. We are not children; I feel what you feel, but will not betray Anne's trust. Our meeting was divine – only someone sent by God would have stopped on a lonely dark and deadly bridge to help a stranded stranger. I am also aware that we have an embarrassing connection, which must be sheathed because I still want to visit here freely without a burdened conscience. To answer your

question, I like you very much – I almost love you; above all,
I appreciate the deep friendship and bond we have." I was
still and tongue-tied; Gloria spoke with such unmistaken affection that it was clear to me that I must pursue her. The fact
that she spoke from her heart without pretenses gladdened my
spirit. The mention of Anne sank my heart because I had for-
gotten that I had a wife. However, I prodded, asking her
views about polygamy and divorce; I was determined to
know her deeper – beyond business. She was 43 years old,
and must desire eventually to settle down; I longed to be the
man she would decide to spend the rest of her life with. I had
come to love and respect her very much…

"Gloria stared unseeing at the television and spoke almost
absent-mindedly, "I am a product of mutual polygamy. My
mother had two of us – my brother and I; birthing me was
complicated delivery which affected my mother's uterus. So,
she could no longer have children. My parents loved children
and had planned on having at least eight before the unfortunate incident. My mother requested my father to marry another wife. The Church excommunicated my parents, because
my mother went ahead to bring in two younger women as
wives. Eventually, seven other siblings came as the young
wives tried to outdo each other in procreation. So, my parents
had a quiver full of us, but we lived happily in love. The
younger wives respected my mother as the Matriarch of family…. That's it for Polygamy. On divorce… it depends. For
example, if Anne sees me in bed with you, she will divorce
you…" We laughed at her last sentence, as I imagined how
Anne would react. Gloria's perspectives to issues were mature, balanced and not sentimental. After a few minutes of

idle talk, we bade each other good night – making sure that there was no contact.

"My children persuaded Gloria not to leave the next day as scheduled; they goaded her into preparing a variety of dishes until Anne's return. She left the next day in the early hours to avoid emotional scenes with the children. I felt like a fish out of water that fateful Sunday and deceived the children that I was ill and could not make it to service. With innocence, they accepted and did their best to take care of me, but I needed to be alone with my thoughts. The mild fragrance from her talcum body spray still assaulted my senses – including the warmth of her breadth from her nostrils as when we hugged. I wondered if it was infatuation or love. I resisted the urge to call her for many days, well aware that she was in constant touch with my children to know how they were doing. I managed to focus on my work, immerse myself in work that had piled due to my trip and lack of attention. My study became my sanctuary, where I could lose myself in work and thoughts about Gloria. After almost a week of her leaving, I summoned courage to call her on a rainy and cold night. She sounded excited and we talked over nothing for close to two hours; she said she was fine and pursuing some business leads to which I made some contributions. Rounding up the conversation, I was tempted to ask the question that had kept me awake most nights. I needed to know if Gloria was thinking about me; her response would give me the lead I so desperately needed. I asked her if she missed me and thought about me even a little; her response welled my heart with desire and love: "Yes, I miss everyone – the children and the house. I miss everything; I missed our little conversations over nothing and have wondered how I could speak about my past so freely with you. Yes, Fred, I almost miss you..." We were silent, filled with irreconcilable emotions; "I am elated hearing that I made the list of the many things that occupied your thoughts..."

"That was the beginning of a love that has blossomed beyond my imagination; I am not infatuated with her; I love Gloria but I cannot throw Anne away. She has many faults, but she is the mother of my children. I have ENDURED our marriage for over a decade as Anne continued to change due to her ambition to climb up the ladder in Banking. The worst period was preparing for her CFA Accounting certification. We operated without a mother and wife because her entire schedules left nothing for us. Marriage means more than bearing the MRS prefix; marriage is a responsibility and divine opportunity to nurture and build character of children. Work priorities must be considered side-by-side family responsibilities and balanced out – and, after 15 maids in 18 years of marriage I can objectively evaluate the difference Gloria made in my home in one week. She reoriented my children towards the path of responsibility and purpose – which continued when she left. We never prayed as a family but today, my daughter takes the lead to ensuring the family gathered for at least five minutes to pray. Anne has not been able to appreciate the transformation in her children and calls my daughter assisting me in the kitchen as 'child abuse'. I have refused to approve another maid being hired into my home; if Gloria could do it, Anne could have tried to sustain the lessons by 'attempting' to do her bit. Anne is too busy to clean, wash, cook or take care of our children. I love taking care of my children; I know she is busy, but this has affected our marriage for years – and my hope of character change from Anne is near zero because she does not even make an effort.

"Nellie, you need to know something: If a woman takes care of her husband, home and children, she closes the doors of opportunities for the devil. I created time to share these with you for clarity and better understanding. I hear Anne on radio and wondered how someone could be so blind to the truth that I am marrying Gloria to help keep my home intact. She once joked that I wanted a maid, derogating the positive attributes of Gloria; that is sad. Gloria is an independent self-made woman who does not need a job to make her fulfilled; she also has a balanced perspective to life. Polygamy is a MUTUAL venture; only understanding between the parties will bring peace at home. My family is aware of my 'trials' in this marriage and cannot help her. On many occasions, my parents wondered why a man would do ALL the chores at home – including sweeping our bedroom and cleaning the bathrooms. Marriage is a partnership, not slavery; there should be mutual respect and understanding. When the under-standing comes from one party alone, it leads to growing ill feelings. I have been on the threshing floor in this marriage of almost two decades; today, I want to live and be happy. A wife that loves her husband should be sensitive enough to know when he is not happy because these moods affect the children.

"There is one more thing I must mention here; the so-called pastors are hypocritical. They do not care about the happiness in you home but in your pocket. I asked my Pastor if his wife behaved like Anne, and he told me "It is well.""

What does that mean? They don't want to offend her because the cheques will drop or reduce. No church member has been honest enough to tell her to study Proverbs 31! This is not a spiritual warfare – it is a clash of commonsense. You can consider it from all angles – culture, scripture and mores – you will come down to the same answer: the need for behavioural change. For this reason, I have stopped going to any church. Nellie let me ask you, "Why did the man after God's heart marry more than one wife? I will tell you… it is because he needed a balance at home as no woman has EVERYTHING it takes to build a successful and peaceful home. You can say these are modern times, but the needs of husbands and children have not changed…. When children don't get love at home – or answers to life's questions – they go outside. More often, the devil is out there to direct them to damnation. The foundation of positive and purposeful living rests with the HOME! Therefore, it is in Anne's best interest to allow us work things out lovingly; alternatively, I could marry Gloria and live with her and my children who already love her very much, but I need my family together and intact… By the way, I already discussed with my children and they are happy that "Daddy is choosing Mummy G as our second mum." She knows Gloria is a very good woman who is also in need of love and companionship; no bad publicity can ruin what we have, and I am trusting God that commonsense will prevail…
"

Sitting there at a famous eatery, listening to him you will observe that Fred was a bundle of conflicting emotions, but spoke from deep within. He seemed to have no pretentions and nothing to hide – he was a man in search of 'love, trust and respect', which are the building blocks of any lasting relationship. He spoke without regrets, rather, with a determination to be happy; surmising his 18 years of marriage to Anne as "wasted years' – the children being the center of his devotion and commitment. It was clear that something was not right. Although every marriage has its challenges, if built on disrespect and dishonor, no degree of hard work would make it right. Fred admitted that in order to build a stable and happy marriage, he stooped subserviently low, as his wife was blinded by career growth, giving near-zero priority to the basics until things began to fall apart.

Sadly, when any man wakes up from 'blind subservience, his reactions can be best imagined. Thus, couples ought to evaluate and reevaluate their relations in an attempt to ensure right balance on every element that forms the union. Wearing the other partner's shoes and views issues from their lenses can aid such a balance. With a very balance view, responding to Anne's letter, capturing issues discussed with the two became less burdensome…

My dearest Anne,
Thank you for the opportunity to discuss your husband's proposed 'Mutual Polygamy'. The subject is delicate and resolution can only be arrived when you, who is at the center of the matter, remove every iota of emotions, taking your personal sentiments out of the picture. This note is actually to further assure that we have clarity and alignment, to enable you take whatever decisions.

When faced with this type of emotional crisis, there is the tendency to view and believe that the 'other woman' is to blame – in this case Gloria. You may need to reconsider, as

Gloria seems to be at the center of something she is entirely innocent of. From your husband's narration, in spite of being friendly with Gloria, who eventually became a family friend and loved by your children, YOU invited Gloria to spend a week in your home during your absence. There were other choices you would have made – our mothers have always filled in for us in 'extreme circumstances'. Your parents live in the same town, so you would have arranged to drop off the kids with them and have a driver take them until Fred's return. You shelved that responsibility to Gloria, and she unselfishly accepted, without any ulterior motive. Gloria would do anything for your family having been saved from the jaws of lion – an event she was repeatedly thankful. So, 'sensing' that your husband had warm feelings towards her, your invitation delivered the meal on a gold platter.

"Mutual Polygamy" is not really a strange concept as Auntie Christy pointed out. However, under the umbrella of a Holy Matrimony in which Fred vowed to keep to only you, mutual polygamy is a juxtaposition of his vow/covenant. Your Aunties (Christy and Jane) are wise women. Only you can decide how to proceed under this strange arrangement. However, these questions are pertinent:

■ Do you love Fred UNCONDITIONALLY to the degree of sharing him with Gloria, to make him happy?

■ Do you feel comfortable being docked by your children who have grown to love and adore Gloria? Children are smarter than we give them credit. They currently refer to Gloria as "Mummy G", and have noted the ease with which their father behaved around her when you were away – and have continued communication with her after your return. How would you manage that? They may be waiting for the right time to ask 'uncomfortable' questions. Are you ready?

■ Do you honestly think you can make a step change and balance duty towards your children and husband with you career? We must sacrifice something at the 'home altar' to please our children and spouse.

■ Fred adores Gloria and said that she is a "wife material" and "angel of my dreams"? This means you are clearly not a 'wife material' – by his calculations. Can you fix this?

Marriage is to be enjoyed, not endured. Fred seemed to have been an 'ENDURING HUSBAND' and posits that his desire to marry Gloria is to bring a balance in the home. Furthermore, it is important to spend time on INTROSPECTION - a period of SELF-SEARCH. My other soul-searching questions for you are:

■ Do you think you have contributed overtly or inadvertently to Fred's 'strange' decision to marry Gloria?

■ Have you honestly been a good and attentive wife?

■ Is your sex life active and healthy? How good is your sex life, really?

■ Do you have a strong bond and friendship that breaks all barriers?

■ Do you spend sufficient time together as a couple?

■ After 18 years of marriage, do you still spark and ignite emotionally without restraint?

■ Are your emotions on lose ends when both of you are alone watching his favourite program?

Note that Fred submitted that Gloria is ingenious with business ideas. Quick question: ***Do you find time to discuss his business or take interest in his struggles?*** The truth is that men emotionally gravitate to anyone who can fill an emotional and rational void. Fred seemed to have been in need of someone who understands his daily struggles as a businessman in an environment that is economically depressed. Gloria comes across as ***a self-assured, defiant and economically independent woman,*** who also understands the challenges of being an entrepreneur. Any man would experiencing emotional drought at home would easily fall for her.

As a Banker, you ought to have understood your husband's challenges better, but Gloria came to fill that 'void' created by you. Sadly, that is the plain, uncoated truth – without sentiments...

I know your heart is broken and you are devastated; however, you need to understand that Fred is being conflicted and considerate at the same time. I know what it means to be in this kind of emotional mess; your heart is torn to shreds from feeling betrayed by the one and only man you have known all your life...Fred feels the same way, too!

You mentioned suicide, and that is sad. One of the things that easily beset us is taking decisions when experiencing emotional stress. During our discussions, we agreed, ***"No one is so important as to make you end your life. You can only destroy what you can create."*** Since your life is sacred and living is not entirely dependent on Fred, it would be most foolish to end your life under these circumstances. Your children will be forever stigmatized by that action… So, perish that thought!!!

My immediate advise is: Take time off on a Personal Retreat. Pool all the issues in a box and work it out alone with God. Only He can give you the Divine Wisdom and Strength to make the right decision. However, you need to understand the emotional dynamics playing around you to enable you make rational life-changing decisions – to either accept *MUTUAL POLYGAMY or MUTUAL DIVORCEMENT.*

Rest assured that whatever your decision, we will continue to connect with you with counseling and prayers. Be good to yourself.

God bless you.
Emotionally Yours

Emotional Piggy Bank
Marriage is a relationship based on the Divine Mathematical Order that the "two shall be one". While love brings them together, there are other fundamental elements that welds the union – "till death do us part". No one can say for sure which ingredients and qualities are guaranteed predictors of a happy and successful marriage. While trust, a similar sense of humour and honesty are judged the three most important factors in a relationship, a few other elements are essential for long-lasting love. However, the best can only come out of understanding individuals and their idiosyncrasies and appreciate their sensitivities. Unfortunately, many couples still struggle

in marriage to understand their spouses.

In the African setting, women are expected to play key roles in determining the longevity of the union. While this perspective have some semblance of truth, the couple have roles to play in ensuring that their relationship is working. Today, the African woman, supporting homes as a breadwinner, faces multiple challenges of balancing career, motherhood and wifely expectations. Due to the exigencies of office work, the tendency to drop the ball at home becomes higher. Thus, every workingwoman needs to adequately focus on quality time management - joggle the balls to ensure no area suffers major impact. Since no one is perfect, a husband's understanding and help will provide the cushion that leads to a balance.

Spousal understanding should not be abused as this can lead to another level of emotional stress, disorientation and crisis in the marriage. Support by any spouse to ensure a balance at home should neither be denigrated nor viewed as a weakness; every helping hand should be appreciated to foster emotional synergy and laughter, which pervade the home with a special aura.

While every marriage is built on trust, respect and honour, **Romance** gives it the required zest and vitality - whether this is a surprise gift, a date night or simply some quality time together.

THE INFLUENCE OF LOVE | Nellie Onwuchekwa

8

Episode 8

Emotional Deception?
Help Me ... I Need My Wife Back!

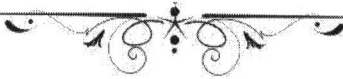

Life is filled with twists and turns. One day it is so perfect and the next, it is all gloomy. But these valleys, cliffs and mountains make life exciting. For some, what I call 'excitement' is emotional stress. Shortly after Anne's *'MUTUAL POLYGAMY'* story was broadcast, 63-year old Chief Willie called us requesting assistance to get his wife back. He loves and dotes on his wife. He should, because Constance, a paradigm of beauty and brains, was 47 years old – 16 years younger than Chief Willie For the purpose of this expose, I want to first submit Willie's perspective in this emotional tango.

About ten years back, Chief Willie, a widower, met 'delectable' Constance who was a Product Marketing Professional. He was cut out of the old stock of money and style - from a 'Wealthy' family – wealthy from every perspective and consideration. Left with four (4) children by his first love, Monique, who died after 'a brief illness', Chief Willie was excited when Constance accepted to marry him.

Constance, a First Class graduate of Economics 'worshipped' as well as 'feared' her husband. She was not allowed to contradict him, otherwise, she would have to face financial sanctions or have some privileges denied. They had been married for about seven (7) years and had a five-year-old son, Brian who Willie loved very much. Willie's other children from Monique were adults and lived on their own. His daughter Yvonne (35) never supported her father's choice, as she wanted her father to either marry a widow or a divorcee with children. Yvonne believed Constance married her father for his money and could not be trusted.

According to Chief Willie, "I know she is having an affair with a younger man because she no longer spends time at home with us (myself and Brian). She comes home late from work daily. When I was very sick and hospitalized, she refused to visit me at the hospital, but travelled to another state for some 'urgent and critical official' work. She does not come into our bedroom anymore, but complains she needs to stay up late to work...I am not a small boy, I know something is wrong. I love my wife, and I need help to get her back".

Willie was really moist speaking with us. To show his desire to get to the bottom of this crisis of confidence and resolve issues with his wife, he gave us Constance's contact details to enable us speak with her.... And we did.

Constance chose a garden located within a popular university to meet with us during her lunch break. Arriving earlier than scheduled, Constance was sighted reading a motivational book. Indeed, Constance was everything her husband described and more. Smartly dressed in a aquamarine blue skirt suit, she was a head turner; young and old turned to look at her glowing skin and radiant smile. We wondered why a paragon of beauty would be involved with someone like Chief Willie. Constance was a little ruffle d when asked to describe her relationship with 'Chief', as she referred to him. She was straight to the point, trying very hard to hold back the tears that welled behind her pupils. The environment helped to restrain her from falling apart; there was no doubt that Constance was in trouble, and she was trying to conceal her deepest emotions from invasion.

Constance confessed she has interests outside her matrimonial home due to "emotional abuse". According to her, Chief Willie continually made reference to "how much he bought the car; how much he bought my hair; how much my allowances are costing him and why I should be glad he married me to get me out of poverty and deprivation."

"My husband makes veiled references to my background.

Yes, I come from a very humble background. Call us poor. Yes, I wanted my family to benefit from the relationship, and Chief has been good to my family. However, his repetitions bother on emotional traumatization and very embarrassing to me. I am emotionally being harassed daily ... I am not happy about the situation. I am not thinking about a divorce because my son is attached to my husband. I am an emotional wreck right now and really confused. Is it a crime to come from a poor background? He chased after me, proposed and eventually married me according to custom; I knew what I was getting into, especially with his educational background. However, I never expected he would turn around to treat me this way. I take good care of him and his needs, and try to be a dutiful wife. Chief knows that there was no love between us, but he promised that it would grow with time. Remember, when agreed to marry Chief, I was running against my biological clock; I prayed to God to send me a husband, and, after over forty years of my life, Chief Willie came, I had to marry him – at least to elevate my family from starvation.

"I care deeply about Willie, but I am not sure I love him in the real sense of the word LOVE; I honestly tried to will myself to love him but to no avail... For me, love died with my first love, Victor, who left me for another woman. I just wanted to have a companion who was older than me and could pamper me like my late father. Chief Willie fitted the bill, but his recent daily disrespect and abuse is driving me mad. I am not an illiterate... I know that his recent health challenges are making him paranoid and creating stories of infidelity where there are none. His daughter is also not helping in this regard. So, to keep my head above this troubled

176

marriage, I had to seek asylum elsewhere – and that is my work!

According to Constance, focusing on her career was a life-saver, as her quarterly rating had continued to go downhill. Due to this poor performance, Constance was assigned a **Mentor/Coach** at her office – as part of Personnel Development program by the Human Resources Department. Her Mentor/Coach, Michael (52) was divorced and lived with his three children. Michael had been a source of encouragement to Constance. He drove Constance harder towards improved productivity and rating to avoid being dropped into the bucket of redundancy and eventual sack list. Between them, personal confidences were shared – and something 'BIG' was beginning to develop between them … gradually.

Constance spoke with candor about her 'involvement' with Michael, but accused her husband for being 'driven into another man's arms'. In her own words: "There is no denying the fact that I find Michael attractive and fun to be with. He respects me and does not judge me. I don't walk or stand on edge when I am with him. He is very supportive professionally and my productivity at work has really improved. He gives me a sense of emotional stability and professional confidence…. Do I love him? I don't know…but he is definitely not a 'fling' guy. *I am looking at a deep friendship. One thing I am sure about is: I don't want to stay with a man who sees me as an ACQUISITION*…. I thought he could change, but he gets worse each day…"

Could lack of sex be the issue? Constance says "Not really…but it is contributory. When you marry, it is for "better" or "worse". If lack of sex is the 'worse' part of your marriage vows due to his health challenge, there are other ways to make up…. *Sex is not everything"*. However, Willie believes that his inability to make love to his wife regularly, and gradual loss of libido is a major factor…

How can we help Chief Willie and Constance regain an emotional balance? Is Michael playing a negative role in this Marriage? Chief Willie's regular emotional abusive seemed to have affected the original bond he had with his wife. Focusing on the age difference and his infrequent libido, Chief Willie was also facing a challenge that he could not freely discuss with friends and family. Incidentally, because of his massive wealth, Chief Willie had lost the commonsense approach to issues – putting his wife constantly down. Lacking humility and a general sense of perspective of what a marriage should be (irrespective of the age gap), he inadvertently pushed his wife to the brink of adultery. Chief Willie believed he loved his wife – his own way – in spite of his shortcoming. He swore that he had been faithful to his wife, who was very loving and caring at the early stages of their marriage, which resulted in the birth of Brian.

Interestingly, Chief Willie believed that the references to his wife's background was to remind her where they started and how he loved her so much he could give her the world – including her parents. He insisted that no other man would marry his wife unless he died, while subtly threatening that any man who attempted marrying Constance would die. *Chief Willie wants his Wife back; but Constance wants her*

Dignity back!!! Constance was experience one of the worst types of abuse – emotional abuses are worse than the physical. While none is desirable, emotional or verbal abuse is intended to humiliate and cause inferiority complex and, in this case, a dependency. Unfortunately, Constance was well aware of that this might happen. No matter how well prepared and kitted for crises, when the time comes, all our response mechanisms fail. This was the case for Constance, who believed she could goad Chief Willie into a marriage of convenience and be able to 'manage the situation', which got out of hand. While Constance had not committed emotionally to Michael, the tendency to fall was quite high. That would be an unkind cut because Michael would end up being her REBOUND.

Constance's struggles are indeed clear; she wants her dignity back. She admitted she made mistakes, but was determined to step out of her mistakes to chart a new course for herself if Willie persists in his ways… The following communications with the couple contributed in resolving the crisis of confidence and eventually averted a major 'war'.

Dear Constance,

*Sessions with you were emotion-laden. We appreciate your openness and honesty on the "emotional entrapment called marriage". We agree you have had a 'frightful' marriage, but it was a relationship **you entered willingly.** You submitted that you did **NOT MARRY FOR LOVE.** That is truly sad for a well-educated young woman of 40 (when you married Willie). An African proverb says: "he who gathers ant-infested firewood should be ready for the dance'. You further admitted that **you married for the money in order to help*** *your family.* *These are the reasons Yvonne and her siblings are wary of you… You sacrificed love on the altar of self-aggrandizement and 'family pressure'. These reasons are enough reasons for Chief Willie's family members to be apprehensive of your 'interest in their son.*

Understandably, Yvonne, your stepdaughter is sensitive about the situation. Daughters have the natural tendency to be over protective of their parents – especially, their father. Thus, you need to understand her and make an effort to reassure her that you truly love and care for her father (if you have eventually grown to love Chief Willie) – to the best of your ability. This is not to suggest that you have to grovel… Always steer the paths of PEACE, as there is never a 'Bad Peace'.

Another issue is Communication. Despite your 'faulty entry' into marriage with Chief Willie, it is expected that communication channels be open between you two. No desperate situation at home should make a wife unable to discuss issues with her husband.

Without sentiments, I hold you responsible for accepting years of emotional abuse, emotional battery and, possibly, physical abuse you suffered in your marriage. Your quest for 'the elegant lifestyle of the wealthy and famous' kept you encapsulated. Rather than make effort to free yourself via counseling, you found an 'escape in work and Michael…" You return daily to a "mansion of agony" to traumatize Chief Willie with jealousy. You seem to have made Michael a pun in this emotional chess game, which is rather unfortunate. This is not fair on Michael who seems ignorant of the reality that you do not love him.

You cannot solve a problem by creating another. Therefore, consider the following:

■ *Introspect and tell yourself the hard truth about your situation;*

■ *A marriage without love is COHABITATION. If that is what you want, accept all the abuses meted out to you because everything has a price;*

■ *Define your relationship with Michael to save him from future heartbreak because he cannot fund your current lifestyle. But, if you love Michael and wish to continue your relationship, please be kind enough to progress dissolution of your union with Willie*

When you take the right steps towards integrity, you will naturally regain your DIGNITY.

Whatever your choice, here is wishing you the best.

Emotionally Yours

Without a shadow of doubt, Chief Willie demonstrated he loved his wife, but was unaware that he was verbally abusing Constance. Jealousy is a negative passion that blinds the individual, driving him or her beyond the plain of reason. Chief Willie exhibited extreme jealousy and further embarrassed Constance by showing up at her place of work to 'demand her faithfulness', thus, widening the communication gap between them. This was a negative move in his desire to regain the love and trust of his wife. With all these play of negative emotions, the atmosphere at home became charged and not conducive for Clarence who always took work home prior to the crisis. Communication gap widened in the storm of suspicion and disrespect…things indeed, fell apart.

After many counseling and mediation sessions, we attempted to capture our thoughts to Chief Willie in the communication below:

Dear Chief Willie,

Thank you for your patience and understanding throughout the 'intrusive' discourse on a matter so sensitive. We only wanted to get facts of the case in order to provide useful feedback without sentiments.

There is no doubt that you 'love' your wife 'very much' – and you want your wife back. It is, however, unfortunate that you seem to speak about your wife like a lost piece of furniture. During the sessions, you talked about "how much it cost me to marry her", "how I have attended to all her needs, without sparing costs', "I give her anything she asks for, no matter how much it costs", "how I have loved and taken care of her family", etc. Little is however said to demonstrate emotional connection, commitment and attention to ensuring emotional stability of your marriage.

You admitted that Constance is 'expected to fear' you as a husband as well as align with your decision on EVERY ISSUE – irrespective of her opinion or perspective. Again, and disappointingly, three (3) years ago, you refused Constance (who has a MBA from a reputable University), not to be involved in the running of your business when she offered her services – to give you the reassurance of her faithfulness. This led to her seeking paid employment elsewhere.

It is important to remind you that marriage is a partnership between two people that love themselves and have committed to live together in love, respect and harmony for the rest of their God-given lives. Regardless of your claim of love for Constance, you did not show an ounce of respect for her. You repeatedly judged Constance using your late wife's standard... "Monique would never do that" reverberated throughout the sessions with you. You cannot slaughter Constance on the altar of your late wife, Monique. This is totally unacceptable and puts your wife under pressure

Husbands are expected to support and encourage their wives to achieve their God-given potential. You see in Constance, your wife, and a Competitor – instead of a HELP-MEET; there is no basis for that. Also, your daughter, Yvonne has a degree of influence on you. There is the need for balance here; Yvonne is married and should have limited involvement in issues between you and Constance. Also, it is pertinent to point out that Constance is YOUR WIFE. Monique, no matter the virtues, is dead.

Consider these Action Steps:
   ■ *Invite your wife and have a discussion (heart to heart); apologize in areas you know you are wrong. Accepting your mistakes is NOT as sign of weakness,*

rather, a show of love and strength.

■ *Ask your wife honestly if your marriage has a future – and show willingness to repair broken bridges/ridges. Listen to Constance with an OPEN HEART & MIND*

■ *Have a session with your daughter, Yvonne. She needs to understand you need Constance. Encourage her to focus on her marriage, while you work things out with Constance.*

■ *Work on the 'challenges' in your sexual relationship with your wife. There are ways to satisfy you both sexually – feel free to ask.*

■ *Upon reconciliation with Constance (God Willing), create a harmonious environment in your home and ensure your children respect YOUR WIFE!!!*

NOTE: You are well aware of the age gap between you and your wife. Age, they say, is a number. However, when there are health challenges, you require love, attention, respect and understanding from your spouse to carry on. Communication is key. Do not stop communicating.

Dear Chief Willie, please separate FAMILY from your marriage. Pursue peace and tread the path of reconciliation. At 63, you need emotional stability, not crisis. You want your wife back, however, Constance wants her DIGNITY back! Can you please take a positive step forward in this direction? Perhaps, you could get your wife back.

Wishing you the best ...

Emotionally Yours

Three months later, the families of Chief Willie and Lady Constance finally reconciled the couple and serenity returned to the mansion. It was interesting to discover that Constance had been holistically faithful to her husband; she had been deeply hurt by the treatment meted out to her by Chief Willie and her stepchildren, and decided to give her husband some distance. The age difference never mattered to her because she walked into the relationship as a full adult as she stated: "I knew the consequences of age-gap. Complicated by his ill health and medications, naturally, his libido is expected to drop. The problem was that Chief felt 'humiliated' whenever he had erectile dysfunction episodes'. I am not a spring chicken too, but there are other ways to fulfill physical sexual desires; he shut all alternatives down!" Chief Willie had concluded that if his beautiful wife was not getting sexual satisfaction from him, then she 'definitely got it from someone out there'. Inadvertently, Michael became their pun...a victim.

Chief Willie was overtaken by emotion as he apologized to his wife, who in turn knelt down and asked for forgiveness for making him jealous and worried about her faithfulness. Yvonne and her siblings, too, were overtaken by guilt and confessed to stoking the fire of hatred and jealousy that drove their father to his 'shameful behaviours towards Constance. According to them, it was difficult to fathom that a beautiful Constance with so much potential could 'actually love' their father unconditionally and remaining faithful 'all this while'.

Unity at the home of Chief Willie and Lady Constance was sealed with a Thanksgiving Service, with Constance appreciated as The Proverbs 31 *'Virtuous Woman'*. That day ,the importance of trust and communication between couples were emphasized; many couples in the church auditorium could be seen nodding and squeezing the hands of their spouses in understanding and remorse… The lessons were clear: Love, trust and respect your spouses, while listening and hearing correctly!!

Emotional Piggy Bank

Overcoming conflicts in marriage is a tough call. Sometimes we don't know what to do to a make amends when we're wrong; other times, we struggle to forgive our spouse when we've been hurt. Conflict is complicated and complex, and most time, very painful. The keys to conflicts in marriage are communication and understanding; even couples with the best literary expertise experience conflicts because they hear but NOT LISTENING to each other. Love has different languages; couples need to understand the language that best relates to their partners and apply as required.

Constance and Willie have misperception challenges that impacted their ability to LISTEN to each other. Mistrust and lack of personal confidence added to the mix and drove them further apart. Thus, it is important to state that relationships can only survive when every element of doubt is banished and couples view each other positively. This increases conviviality that adds to the fragrance of romance in every relationship.

Have faith in your partner and the doubt will flee; avoid creating a distance because you will be inviting a 'third party' into your home. Perhaps the guidance for all couples on the benefits of love and positive emotions in relationships are best captured by masterfully crafted Poem, *'Love At Home'* by John H. McNaughton (1854), which still remains one of the most powerful songs for joining and blessing couples during the nuptials:

1 There is beauty all around,
When there's love at home;
There is joy in every sound,
When there's love at home;
Peace and plenty here abide,
Smiling sweet on every side,
Time doth softly, sweetly glide,
When there's love at home.

2. In the cottage there is joy,
When there's love at home;
Hate and envy ne'er annoy,
When there's love at home;
Roses bloom beneath our feet,
All the earth's a garden sweet,
Making life a bliss complete,
When there's love at home.

3. Love becomes a way of life,
When there's love at home;
Sweet, insistent end to strife,
When there's love at home;
Glad submission each one's gift,
Willing pledge to love and lift,

187

Healing balm for every rift,
When there's love at home.

4. Anger cools and pressures cease,
When there's love at home;
Children learn to live in peace,
When there's love at home;
Courage to reach out in grace,
Meet a stranger face to face,
Find a reconciling place,
When there's love at home.

5. There's no question you can't ask,
When there's love at home;
There is strength for any task,
When there's love at home;
Sharing joy in work or play,
Confidence to face the day,
Knowing love will find a way,
When there's love at home.

6. Kindly heaven smiles above,
When there's love at home;
All the world is filled with love,
When there's love at home;
Sweeter sings the brooklet by,
Brighter beams the azure sky;
Oh, there's One who smiles on high
When there's love at home.

Epilogue

Reflections:
Emotional Complexities

In life, we traverse thousands of emotional lines; we carry unimaginable tons of emotional debris, and we inadvertently weather through every storm like a troubadour. Each waking moment is like holding on to the lifesaver rope that swings us to safety. Sometimes hopeful, and, other times, very despondent; yet we try to smile, to live and to ensure that our trips are marked in the sands of times. The complexities of relationships sometimes overwhelm us – and other times, we overwhelm life by the inner deposits from on high.

Every individual is an entangled mess, but God provides a way of emotional escape. When trapped in the holes of dejection and depression, an inner voice call us forth to sail through the storms of emotional crises. Yes, we have had some! No man or woman is free of this natural strengthener called emotions – we are complete after the roll in the storm of emotions. Yes, without it we are at best emotional toddlers. We yearn for emotional independence, but the Creator has ensured a natural mutation into emotional dependence – for we must RELATE! Yes, RELATE. Relationships are emotions-dependent because that aids our completion.

Some have experienced the worst of them all, and conceded emotional defeat and resting in the nest of emotional despondency. Some have crawled out of that despondent nest to emotional triumph – they struggled with the worst animals in the jungle of emotions, of love, and of betrayal and stayed steadfast to the calling to emotional maturity and reliance. For, they will not bow to a life of emotional mediocrity – for such would mean a life not worth living. So, they continue to walk the tiresome journey to that 'safety nest' of emotional convergence, which gives you peace, yes, peace in the midst of the storms.

Yes, I traversed and did see the weak become emotional giants; yes, seated on the *'Emotionally Yours'* Counseling Seat, watching, scribing, praying and yearning for a soothing closure, I did see the influence of love reigning supreme and triumphant. Sometimes, it became an invasion of the soul – the soul searching, the complexities of emotional transition from love to hate and back to unconditional love. Many emotional pendulums did swing uncontrollably! Indeed, God created masses of tissues that overwhelm every scientist and psychologist.

Flashing back to that Philosophical Foundation class at the University of Lagos, Akoka, Yaba, Lagos, Nigeria, with beloved Late Rev. Father Schyler, I mentally scan my famous philosophers and wonder if they did enough to capture the essence of emotions and love. Incidentally, many philosophers ended emotionally impoverished by overly philosophizing the issue instead of providing 'experiential philosophy' like King Solomon's emotional well treatise captured in **Songs of Solomon.** They forget that the essence of philosophy is based on experiential triumphs – overcoming the potholes in the path to emotional maturity and balance. Something was missing in their lives – for many died in emotional despondency or afraid to escape the bed and nest of solitude. Sad.

Today, we see men and women scampering into unimaginable shelters at the mention of "LOVE" - they cannot deal with emotional issues. They are emotionally spent! Unfortunately, in the dead hours of the night, nay, in the still hours of the night, through the dawn of a new day, they wonder what is missing in their lives; they extend their hands to each end of the bed to meet cold pillows. Oh, how they wished to reach out to warm flesh! Some have become averse to their bedrooms, preferring to stay on their cozy lounges in the living rooms, only to be greeted by alarms in cold hours of the morning. They reach out for a hot cup of tea or coffee, when they actually needed the **WARM HUG** of a loved one with a "Good Morning" so well deserved.

We are all Epicureans. Life may bend and twist us undeservedly, but love and positive emotions influence our receptors to overcome and reinvigorate. Thus, to survive is to be emotionally balanced; to live is to emotionally transit from the whirlpool of despondency to maturity and triumph. Yes, we have the emotional potential to leap through all emotional storms to the safe haven that only **TRUE LOVE** can transit us. Doubts abound, and must be vanquished because it is a deadly virus that terminates every relationship. Doubts are only potent in destruction. For, as we demonstrate 'faith' in an alarm clock to wake us at dawn or specific tasks; we must in the same manner wake up to the realities that we are created RELATIONAL BEINGS – and have FAITH in the Divine Scientist Who dexterously gathered each tissue to speak of a need, a yearning and eventual settling.

We are all in search of our **MATURITY EMOTIONAL NEST** – decidedly or inadvertently. Only true love and positive emotions can transform a BEAST to a genteel soul. Every good emotion is transformational, leading towards the positive. Period. Sometimes, we delude ourselves that we are complete without that 'emotional counterpart' that holds the last sinews to mark our completeness. We are emotionally arrogant and deny the need to emotionally vent, connect and complete the search of the missing compass.

Everyone lacking emotional maturity and stability is still paddling the boat in search of the missing component. Sometimes, in arrogance, we settle for wrong compass and are navigated into the spheres in which we feel emotionally bereft and juxtaposed. Naturally, we try to mix iron and clay and pray that thy weld; unfortunately the mix is not natural, hence, the eventual disintegration. Then we begin another lap in search of the 'right' materials that cause the right mix. This is our natural emotional mutation towards a place of emotional settlement. It is not the money or the fame; it is the convergence of the right variables that make the WHOLE.

What does this mean to us? We can only find peace when the right mix has been achieved. Some get it right at start up, while others are able to fix it midlife – some ensure they get it right during the last lap of their journeys on earth. Whether we accept it or not, emotional traversing is natural because we gravitate towards variables that give us peace…and that is emotional stability, leading to emotional maturity. To stabilize, our emotions go up in storm-fit until it settles in the brook of emotional serenity. That is peace, happiness and self-actualization.

Only then is the influence of love and triumphant made manifest!

Nellie Roselynde Onwuchekwa

■ Nellie Roselynde Onwuchekwa, B.Sc. M.ILD, is Vice President of US-based Guardian Solutions and Group Chief Executive Officer of Afresh Group in Nigeria. An entrepreneur and philanthropist, Nellie is the founder of Afresh Global Foundation and Chief Sponsor of 'Emotionally Yours Show' and 'Growth Café Seminars', which has provided learning for over 10,000 youths annually. She has continued to provide professional guidance and support for victims of emotional trauma.

Man is a bundle of emotions. Our Emotions play critical roles on how we think and behave – and respond to stimulus or events around us. Different interplays of elements impact our emotional responses, and influence the outcome of our relationships. Incidentally, emotions can be really complex, and, response to emotional stimuli – rational or irrational, may have life-changing impact on our lives. The Influence of Love broadens the reader's perspectives on complexities of Love and emotions; and offers positive resolution paths.

Written in episodes, this book uses true-life events to invoke the power of INFLUENCE in emotional entanglements. Passages accentuate the powerful dynamics of INFLUENCE, which directly affects decisions of partners in relationships. Each episode reflects individual emotional struggles, conflicts, and sometimes, painful resolution processes. Of great importance is the author's key principle that "a relationship without invisible underpinning influencing variables is chaff at best". Enjoy exploring the depth of pain, emotion, pleasure, and rationality that form the building blocks of stable relationships via the Influence of Love.

Nellie Roselynde Onwuchekwa, B.Sc. M.ILD, is Vice President of US-based Guardian Solutions and Group Chief Executive Officer of Afresh Group in Nigeria.

An entrepreneur and philanthropist, Nellie is the founder of Afresh Global Foundation and Chief Sponsor of 'Emotionally Yours Show' and 'Growth Café Seminars', which has provided learning for over 10,000 youths annually.

Nellie Roselynde Onwuchekwa, B.Sc. M.ILD, is Vice President (Busi-

ness Development) of US-based Guardian Solutions and Group Chief Executive Officer of Afresh Group in Nigeria. A Security and Risk Management Expert, Nellie spent 20 years managing threat matrixes, business integrity, compliance issues and environmental complexities in the Oil and Gas industry for Mobil Producing Nigeria, an ExxonMobil Subsidiary in Nigeria. Dealing with in Business Continuity Planning and Execution, Process and Compliance, Risk Management, Security Surveying and Designs, Project Management Assessment, Due Diligence Investigations and Personnel Background Vetting provided the basis for issues-centered 'emotional escape program' – the 'Emotionally Yours Show' on UNILAG FM. During the last ten years, Nellie has been committed to emotional counseling and supporting families undergoing various levels of emotional crisis.

An entrepreneur and philanthropist, Nellie is the founder of Afresh Global Foundation and Chief Sponsor of 'Emotionally Yours Show' and 'Growth Café Seminars', which has provided learning for over 10,000 youths annually. She has continued to provide professional guidance and support for victims of emotional trauma. Communications Director for Western Nigeria Union Conferences and Board Member of Adventist Development and Relief Agency (ADRA) Nigeria, Nellie Onwuchekwa's commitment to the development of Nigerian youth remains unparalleled.

AMERICAN
JOURNAL *of*
TRANSFORMATIONAL
LEADERSHIP

Made in the USA
Columbia, SC
08 February 2018